1/10-4y

East Meadow Public Library
1886 Front Street
East Meadow, New York 11554
516-794-2570
www.eastmeadow.info

JEWISH ENCOUNTERS

Jonathan Rosen, General Editor

Jewish Encounters is a collaboration between Schocken and
Nextbook, a project devoted to the promotion of Jewish literature, culture, and ideas.

PUBLISHED

FORTHCOMING

The Jewish Body

MELVIN KONNER

THE JEWISH BODY

NEXTBOOK · SCHOCKEN · NEW YORK

Copyright © 2009 by Melvin Konner

All rights reserved. Published in the United States by
Schocken Books, a division of Random House, Inc., New York,
and in Canada by Random House of Canada Limited, Toronto.

Schocken Books and colophon are registered trademarks of
Random House, Inc.

Library of Congress Cataloging-in-Publication Data
Konner, Melvin.
    The Jewish body / Melvin Konner.
    p. cm.—(Jewish encounters)
    Includes index.
    Includes bibliographical references and index.
    ISBN 978-0-8052-4236-2
    1. Body, Human—Religious aspects—Judaism.
2. Body, Human, in literature. 3. Body, Human—Social
aspects. 4. Body, Human, in the Bible. 5. Body, Human, in
rabbinical literature. 6. Jews—Identity. 7. Race.
8. Stereotypes (Social psychology). 9. Body image—Social
aspects. I. Title.
                BM627 K65 2008
                296 3'2—dc22
                2008017625

www.schocken.com
Printed in the United States of America
First Edition
2 4 6 8 9 7 5 3 1

TO MY CHILDREN
Susanna, Adam, and Sarah
AND TO THEIRS

CONTENTS

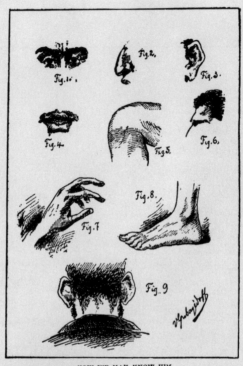

HOW WE MAY KNOW HIM.

Fig. 1. Restless suspicious eyes.	**Fig. 5.** Round knees.
Fig. 2. Curved nose and nostrils.	**Fig. 6.** Low brow.
Fig. 3. Ill-shapen ears of great size like those of a bat.	**Fig. 7.** Long clammy fingers.
Fig. 4. Thick lips and sharp rat's teeth.	**Fig. 8.** Flat feet.
	Fig 9. Repulsive rear view.

A nineteenth-century guide to identifying Jews.
Courtesy of the New York Public Library, Astor, Lenox, and Tilden Foundations. Used by permission of NYPL Photographic Services & Permissions.

PREFACE

There is an illustration, an informative chart in fact, reprinted in a book called *Kike! A Documentary History of Anti-Semitism in America*. The chart was first published in 1888 in a book called *The Original Mr. Jacobs*, by the noted author "Anon." It consists of nine small pen-and-ink drawings of body parts, with a helpful legend keyed to them. It is called "How We May Know Him," and the legend says:

> Fig. 1 Restless suspicious eyes. Fig. 2 Curved nose and nostrils. Fig. 3 Ill-shapen ears of great size like those of a bat. Fig. 4 Thick lips and sharp rat's teeth. Fig. 5 Round knees. Fig. 6 Low brow. Fig. 7 Long clammy fingers. Fig. 8 Flat feet. Fig. 9 Repulsive rear view.

Figure 2 is a classic side view of the Jewish nose, Figure 4 displays the rat's teeth between fleshy lips, Figure 7 looks more like a claw than a hand, and Figure 9, a rear view of the subject, shows just huge ears and a hairy neck. The Nazi view of Jewish anatomy would actually be much more subtle and scientific, but after all, it was half a century later and in the world's most civilized nation, not that primitive backwater America. Still, although the Germans could build on work done in America and Europe throughout the nineteenth century, the foundations go much deeper, and it is part of this book's purpose to trace them.

But it will do much more than depict the Jewish body from the viewpoint of its enemies. Since ancient times, Jews have had very clear ideas about their own bodies, and these ideas—and the practices that went along with them—changed dramatically over the three millennia since the Jews became an identifiable people. Some had to do with regulating sex, some involved internalizing contemptuous images drawn by others, some were deliberate reactions against those images, and some involved what might be called a centuries-long compare-and-contrast exercise between the Jewish body and the body (if any) of the Jewish God.

Jews are known as the people of the book, but they have also been called the people of the body,[1] and some of their most revered books through the ages have dealt extensively with the body—how and how not to change it, care for it, reproduce it, satisfy its insistent demands, bless and thank God for its myriad functions, and dispose of it after all those functions cease. The Hebrew Bible is full of messages about the body and twenty centuries of rabbinical interpretations of them have parsed them to the nth degree. The Jewish body during those centuries went from strong and warlike to weak and submissive and back to strong and warlike again, with momentous consequences for Jewish destiny.

As for God's body, Jewish destiny was shaped by the Jews' insistence that God didn't have one, yet their refusal to embody God was inextricably tied up with their views about their own bodies. The medieval mystic books of the Kabbalah tried to give God a body after all and scholars have argued over its meaning ever since. Jacob, who *is* Israel, "wrestled with gods and men and won," although he limped away, so the people of the book are also called God-wrestlers. In the last century or so, some Jewish writers have shown less interest in wrestling with God than with the world and with themselves, and their ideas about the Jewish body, some ironic and funny, some rude and bawdy, some tragic and grotesque, have shaped the consciousness of countless readers, Jewish and non.

It is my goal in this book not only to trace the Jewish body through its radical, almost magical transformations, but to try to understand how Jewish bodies and Jewish thoughts about them have shaped the Jewish mind and the Jewish contribution to civilization. Finally, very tentatively and carefully, we will consider how centuries of relative bodily isolation, inspired for better or worse by ideas about the body, may have shaped Jewish genes. If there is a thread that organizes all these themes, it is this: The world made the Jews weak, so weak for so long that even *they* became convinced that the only strength they would ever have would be mental. That sort of strength they had in ample measure, and they used it to refine their approaches to God and human, male and female, sex and love, tragedy and comedy into an exquisite array of comforting distractions. They came, however, to mistrust the physical, so much so that their bodies seemed both polluting and comical to themselves and others. The comedy offered relief, as did the comfort of sexuality, and we will see how. So did the Torah, for the many who embraced it.

But two great events of the twentieth century—one the worst thing that ever happened to the Jews, and the other the best—turned the tables on Jewish weakness forever. Strength prevailed, because the very best powers of the Jewish mind became allied to a new physical strength, rising out of the ashes and blood of six million murders. This synergy produced the state and the army of Israel. It has won, and will continue to win, great victories against great odds.

As I was growing up, my beloved rabbi, Bernard L. Berzon, delivered passionate sermons about Torah, ethics, and observance, but also about Israel. One of them, collected in his book *Good Beginnings*, was on the Torah passage in which Moses, in his first act of solidarity with his people, kills an Egyptian who is brutally beating a Hebrew slave. The rabbi referred to the *galut*, the exile, which followed centuries later and lasted for millennia.

"Through the centuries of dispersion and exile, the Jew developed a *galut* psychology of fear and, like his ancestors in Egypt, yielded to the onslaughts and insults of vicious men in a degrading and humiliating manner. He bent to receive the kicks and blows of every murderous charlatan without fighting back. He practiced the policy of nonresistance long before Ghandi and Nehru. He became spineless and frail—afraid to strike back. Those who spent their early youth in Europe will bear me out that this was generally the case. When an anti-Semitic scoundrel threatened one of our people, the Jew would either run for his life, beg for mercy, or cover his face with his hands to ward off the blows."

There were many in our synagogue to bear him out, and I often heard their stories. But on that Saturday morning, this is what they and I heard next: "We in our generation have lived to witness the rebirth of Jewish courage. Thank God that our sons and daughters in Israel have learned to use their fists against their foes . . . Blessed be the fist of each one of our heroes! May they continue to use their hands against the would-be annihilators of Israel."

The Jews tried mind alone for eighteen hundred years; that led to defenselessness, contempt, isolation, pogroms, and finally mass murder on a scale unknown in human history. The traditional balms of God, law, ritual, learning, love, sex, family, narrative, and comedy passed through the gates of Auschwitz and were all found wanting. God did not answer the prayers of the victims, the Torah did not explain their plight, their sense of humor slammed into a burning wall. Enforced starvation and pestilence abolished sexuality, and married women were shot for the crime of pregnancy. One and a half million children were murdered; the love of their mothers and fathers did not save them. Survival on this planet depends not on mind alone, but on mind and body, argument and physical force, learning and fighting, genius and, yes, violence judiciously construed. The world has been, is, and will be a very dangerous place for Jews. They tried weakness—oh, how they tried; indeed, they were better versed in it than anyone else on earth. Strength is better.

The Jewish Body

PROLOGUE

Growing up in the 1950s, I was a more or less normal adolescent boy, which in itself entails a lot of anatomical curiosity, and since I was amply familiar with my own body, I was eager to know more about the fairer sex—or more exactly, the sex of the fairer sex. In the timid fifties, we were not exactly flooded with the facts of life. No sex ed courses, no explicit talk on TV, no graphic rappers naming forbidden organs, no movies leaving nothing to even the wildest imaginations. We were not only starved for sex, we were desperately scrounging for scraps of knowledge about it.

But I wasn't just an average boy of the fearful fifties, I was Orthodox. From the first hot blast of puberty I wanted to be pure but was not getting even close, and God was reading my filthy mind every minute of every day—not to mention the frustrated nights. Psychologists find that girls going through puberty experience anxiety and even depression over their changing bodies and body images; like most boys, in contrast, I couldn't wait to leave my childish body behind.

I was soft and pudgy. "Husky," they called it then, in the boys' pants department where, to my mortification, my mother had to take me. I was terrible at team sports, although I did try, sometimes to the dismay of captains of stickball or punchball teams, who eventually had to pick me, too, for our street games. I did well in school, Hebrew school, and even the Boy Scouts, which—even though it was a Jewish troop that met in the synagogue basement—I dearly hoped was going to toughen me up a little, so that I wouldn't fall quite so far short of the American manly ideal.

Not that there weren't models among the Jewish men. Some had just returned from World War II combat. Others, new Americans, bore blue tattooed numbers on their forearms. One short, solidly muscular, very handsome forty-ish man with graying curly hair—I can still see him striding confidently along the stained-glass windows, backlit by sunlight filtered through his prayer shawl—was said to have gone to the gas chambers three times, each time breathing the air in a space beneath the falling bodies. Then, too, there was a refugee from a different era, squat, bent, and elderly with only a few remaining strands of white hair, who had survived Russian pogroms at the turn of the century. He was missing the first joint of his right index finger—his trigger finger—because he had deliberately cut it off to avoid serving in the tsar's army, at a time when you were drafted for twenty-five years.

Two of my uncles had fought in France in World War I. And there was my cousin, after whom I was named, serenely handsome in his hometown newspaper photo, wearing his Army Air Corps captain's uniform, protected from age by death. He'd been downed by lightning as the copilot of a B–25 bomber when he was just about to be shipped overseas.

These and many other Jewish men's bodies fascinated me, and I wished I could be like them. In my fantasy life I was leading the escape from the concentration camp or piloting the bomber, winning the war against Hitler and shutting down the gas chambers. But I wasn't like them. For one thing, I wasn't going through puberty fast enough, and one of my nicknames in the Boy Scouts was "Baby Fat," which at least had a kernel of hope in it, since normal growth might make it go away, and maybe with it my shyness. I went through the tortures of the damned before I could raise my hand in class. The last thing I wanted to do was call attention to my body.

For most of my childhood I had been in the synagogue every day of the week, yet as a teenager I became steadily *more* religious. I lacked the courage to wear a yarmulke to public school, but I began to put it on as soon as I got home. To my parents' puzzlement, I unscrewed the bulb in the refrigerator before sunset on Friday, making my father grope in the dark for his midnight snack. And, after my bar mitzvah, I began to put on tefillin and *daven* every morning at home. *How goodly are thy tents, O Jacob, thy dwelling places, O Israel!* This took me back in an instant to ancient times, when God was clearly and constantly present among the Jews, a time of heroes, of Jewish glory. I went on to intone the prayer about the body, just awakened from the almost deathly, awesome state of sleep:

Blessed art Thou O Lord our God, King of the universe, Who has formed man in wisdom, and created in him many passages and vessels. It is well known before Thy glorious throne, that if but one of these be opened, or one of those be closed, it would be impossible to exist and stand before Thee. Blessed art Thou O Lord, Who heals all flesh and works wonders. For a sleepy, pudgy boy whose body was not a source of pride or even pleasure, it was a comforting way to start the day.

And then there was the litany of other blessings, many of which were about the body: *Blessed art Thou O Lord our God, King of the universe . . .*

. . . *Who opens the eyes of the blind.*

. . . *Who clothes the naked.*

. . . *Who girds Israel with might.*

. . . *Who gives strength to the weary.*

. . . *Who removes sleep from my eyes and slumber from my eyelids.*

And then, too,

. . . *Who has not made me a heathen.*

. . . *Who has not made me a slave.*

. . . *Who has not made me . . . a woman.*

I said this, while women, I knew, said *Who has made me according to Thy will.* Evasive explanations notwithstanding, the message was clear even to a boy.

But if not being a woman made me special, surely the thoughts and feelings I was having about women had to be somehow part of God's plan for me. Yet Bonnie Gitlin, a seventh-grade goddess with a cloud of blond curls and (already!) actual breasts, took no notice of me or my crush on her, even though I sat right behind her in homeroom. Except once when I tripped sidling between the rows as we filed in for auditorium, and I saw her grin and call me "Klutzy" to one of her entourage. In what was surely blasphemy even to a God whose first commandment was *Be fruitful and multiply,* I began to wrap my tefillin especially tightly around my forearm, so the indentations the leather left on my skin would last longer. I would get to homeroom and the stripes would still be faintly there. Perhaps Bonnie would notice them one day and ask me about them. After that anything might be possible. Needless to say, this was not the right pickup strategy for Bonnie, nor were any of my other ideas about courtship over the next couple of years. My late-night reveries became ever more frustrated. Yet I couldn't find out almost anything in those benighted days about the subject that interested me most.

Imagine my surprise and delight when I and a couple of other boys began to study Talmud with the rabbi's son—an aspiring rabbi himself—after my high school day was over: The first of the twenty-odd volumes we dipped into was opened to an order—that's what the Talmud's six main sections are called—with the marvelous title of *Nashim*, which just means "Women." My search, I thought, was over, and it had ended in the most unlikely place.

Nashim records the opinions and debates of rabbis (what the Talmud basically consists of) concerning the very subject I aspired to study and master. So here we were, a bunch of adolescent boys sitting around a table pondering the revered expert opinions of a bunch of ancient (both senses of the word) *men* who sat around *their* table pondering that mysterious, intricate, unplumbed subject, "Women." Like me, apparently, the rabbis of old were beset with anatomical curiosity, but they legitimized and even sacralized it by debating what the Torah had meant to say about women.

The first few of the eight tractates, or subsections, of *Nashim* dealt basically with the laws about who could marry or divorce whom, when and how, and what obligations were entailed in matrimony. These contracts were not without interest. In the marriage contract, for instance, a man's obligations to his wife were (and are) clearly spelled out: food, clothing, and sex. All right, I thought; the revered rabbis not only okayed it, they required it—although from what I saw in high school (not to mention what I felt in my own Jewish body), it seemed odd to imply, as the rabbis sometimes did, that sex was something *women* need and men provide out of a sense of obligation.

I later discovered that the rabbis' views were a lot more complex. Roaming around in the Talmud—especially with the English translation on the facing page, a very long shelf of books—produced many discoveries. *Taharot*, or "Purity," contained a tractate called *Niddah*, which meant "Menstruating Woman"—yucky but fascinating. Interested as I was in high school biology, it had so far all been frog dissections and smelly paramecium cultures. Now my religious studies were getting me inside women's bodies, legitimizing my interest in their mysterious machinery. Menstrual blood made women impure, to be sure, as did intermenstrual bleeding and even childbirth itself. But after the time of impurity, a woman immersed herself in the *mikvah*, the ritual bath, and became pure again, which meant her husband could once again have sex with her.

The laws about women's bodies represent no more than a fraction of the vast reaches of the Talmud, a great compendium of wisdom, judgment, philosophy, tradition, story, and law. As much as anything it was what sustained the Jewish people for two millennia. Still, for a boy wondering rather desperately about all the secrets of women and sex, it seemed legitimate now to be curious about these things, because the greatest rabbis who ever lived were curious about them, too.

Not only that, they were, like me, quite capable of the lewdest thoughts. This is made explicit and a cornerstone of Jewish law: All men are lustful, and therefore no man, even if his occupation takes him among women, is allowed to be in their presence unless one of them is his wife or a close relative. Talmud stories convey critical lessons, and the ones about rabbis facing temptation are some of the most telling.[1]

Rav and Rabbi Judah are walking behind a woman when Rav says they must pass her so as not to become aroused. Judah reminds him that he has ruled that "fit men" could be in the presence of women. "I did not mean fit men like you and me," Rav replies; though they are among the greatest of rabbis, neither is fit to control his lust.

Amram the Pious finds himself in the awkward position of having some women redeemed from captivity staying temporarily in an upper floor of his house. Ten strong men remove the heavy ladder so that no man can get up there. But Rabbi Amram catches a glimpse of one of the women and finds the strength to move the ladder back by himself. Halfway up the ladder his conscience pricks him and he cries out, "Fire at Rabbi Amram's!" Other rabbis run to his house and save Amram from his own incendiary desire.

Rabbi Meir and Rabbi Akiva are two of the greatest

sages, yet each has Satan appear to him as a beautiful woman. Meir spies his across a river and, there being no ferry at the time, starts to pull himself across with the ferry rope. Akiva (who famously married a peerless wife for love) sees his own temptress atop a palm tree, which he starts to climb. But in each case the Satanic lovely is warned off by a voice from Heaven, *Beware of the rabbi and his Torah!* and lets the straying sage go.

And Rabbi Hiya, tormented by sexual urges, ascetically keeps himself from his wife until out of frustration and loneliness she disguises herself as a prostitute and comes to him in his garden. He propositions her, she makes him fetch a pomegranate from the very top of the tree, and they couple. Coming home to his wife as herself, he confesses and crawls inside the oven. Her explanation (and proof, with the pomegranate) is to no avail. What she meant as a lesson to mend his ascetic ways leads to still greater guilt as he torments and fasts himself to death.

So the rabbis, far from considering themselves above temptation, count themselves among the greatest sinners. Yet desire is normal—that is why men must marry—and Hiya's first mistake is to fail to have sex with his wife. The message is that all men are imbued with very strong sexual urges that cannot be suppressed, only channeled, and the whole point of the Rabbinic debates and laws about men and women is to help us with the channeling. Even as a boy I understood this, and I tried to live up to what my beloved rabbi, and the millennial succession of his teachers before him, expected of me.

S till, at the age of seventeen, I lost my faith. I started college that fall, still living at home with my parents, who were poor enough that tuition-free Brooklyn College—whose clock-tower spire I had gazed at from my childhood bedroom window—was really my only choice. Fortunately it was a good one, but there were other things going on in my life and in the world besides a college education. In August, still sixteen by a few days, I defied my parents to go to Washington, where I heard Martin Luther King Jr. deliver the speech that would change America and the world. White as I was (to whatever extent Jews are really white), his dream was my dream, too. I was active in that movement, in the grassroots effort to stave off nuclear war (a constant threat in that dangerous era), and was already protesting the small but growing American involvement in Vietnam.

In philosophy class I sat next to a beautiful girl with pale skin and eyes and long dark hair who won my heart. The professor would come in, sit cross-legged on the desk, blow pipe smoke in our direction, and start "doing philosophy," which in his case meant, among other things, undermining faith with the power of language analysis. Still an Orthodox Jew, I had little use for this, and frequently succumbed to the temptation to whisper with my pale-eyed friend. Halfway through the semester, the prof—quite properly—called us up after class and asked us to sit separately. In a huff, I stopped coming, and ended with a D+.

But his message must have sunk in somehow, or else I

must have been ready for it. For most of the semester I walked to that young woman's house, almost an hour each way, on Friday nights to observe the Sabbath. By the end of that term (I lost the girl to another boy) I was no longer a believer. I decided to study anthropology to get a new take on religion and a new story of the human past. I was premed, like every other good Jewish boy in that era, but I pursued another path of curiosity, regarding human nature and its origins. I went to graduate school in biological anthropology and learned about the biological bases of human behavior—the embodiment of mind.

I spent two years doing research among hunters and gatherers in Africa's Kalahari Desert, and taught about anthropology and human nature for five years, when my more basic, older anatomical curiosity finally overcame me, and I did go to medical school. My favorite saying, *Nothing human is alien to me*, now meant not just the Kalahari hunter-gatherers but every conceivable physical and mental illness, as well as the "normal" processes of birth (I delivered thirty-five babies) and death.

I finished medical school but went back to teaching. Because of Africa, because of medicine and illness, and not least because of fatherhood, I was a changed man, but I was just as obsessed as ever about the body. I thought I was finished with anything very explicitly Jewish, but I could hardly have been more wrong, and it was the tiny body of my first child, a daughter, and the expectant look in her eyes, that let me know in no uncertain terms that Judaism and Jewishness were not finished with me.

1

God's Body

A *god without a body.* From the beginning, this peculiar, even crazy notion anchored the faith of the Jews and made them objects of ridicule and suspicion among their neighbors. So strange was this idea that their own prophets had to pound them with it because of their persistent drift back toward idolatry. Much later it divided them from Christians, too—a process going on today as Jews watch Christians lament the mortification of Christ and mysteriously consume his body and blood. The ancient Greeks (who had, we will see, a cult of the body) called them atheists, since evidence of their faith, in the usual wood and stone forms, was nil.

Their altars in temples on high places were certainly made for sacrifice—on festival days, the blood of sheep and goats ran down like streams. But what were they sacrificing *to*? Where was the gorgeously crafted graven image that for every normal people showed not only what the gods looked like but also which in that particular place and time would have his or her nostrils filled with the sweet aroma of all those burnt offerings?

Household figurine of the Canaanite goddess Ashera.
Courtesy of Sacred Source/Ancient Images Ancient Wisdom,
www.sacredsource.com. Used by permission.

Despite variations from culture to culture, everyone knew what the gods were: greatly enhanced versions of men, women, or animals, with human and superhuman natures. They had special bodies, no doubt. They could make their bodies invisible, transport them from heaven to earth in an instant, appear as beggars or soldiers, change themselves into the huge, strong bodies of bulls or the elegant bodies of swans, or replace their human heads with heads of elephants. They were immortal, mysterious, and unbelievably endowed, but they were unquestionably embodied. The oldest fertility goddesses were gravid with fat thighs and bellies, the later ones lithe sexual beauties, a messenger god was fleet of foot, a sex god was half randy bovine, and the goddess of intelligence was born out of the very head of the father of all the other gods.

And here now was this weak, primitive, upstart, annoying Johnny-come-lately people, country bumpkins, really, who could build practically nothing and rarely won a war, come toddling along to tell the world's great civilizations that you shouldn't carve or hammer out an image of a god, and furthermore, there was only *one* of them! Not surprisingly, many Jews didn't believe this themselves but hid and hoarded household carvings in wood, stone, and precious metals, some even assembled from stuck-together lumps of crockery, while their priests and prophets railed against them, trying to make them worship *only* a body-less, invisible, unitary god. An abstraction. A figment, perhaps, of prophetic or priestly imagination. A disembodied voice booming out of a cloud or a bush. A ghostly, forceful, collective memory. An all-knowing, all-seeing, all-thinking mind, with a capital M if you like, but a mind only.

No wonder these Jews were called atheists. No wonder the common people among them longed for and clung to the old gods with arms and heads and torsos, with male and female gender, with transcendent beauty or a twisted, gimpy leg, with speed or strength, with a superhuman capacity to feel and survive physical pain. No wonder that, in the prophets' words, this "stiff-necked people" constantly slid back.

No wonder, either, that, even as they lost their last temple and became, willy-nilly, *more* abstract, even as they shaped a new version of their religion without the ritual slaughter of live animal bodies, without an altar or a temple, with basically nothing but texts and conversations describing their great invisible God—a student of Aristotle's wrote of the Jews, "Philosophers by race, they converse with each other about their God"—they spawned a new daughter religion, Christianity, which returned to the body, literally, with a vengeance. The bodiless Jewish God, according to new doctrine, had sent a sacred spirit to impregnate a thoroughly *human* being, a woman—however holy—going from dust to dust, and in her womb sprang up a physical embodiment of God himself, a paradoxical son of God who was also God, a part of God that would assume a truly human form, be born in pain and risk and blood, grow up under stress and prejudice, breathe, eat, drink, eliminate, and feel a beating human heart in an all-too-human breast. And this man, this body inhabited by God, would suffer and sense not only the pain of every other human being but the most extreme pain that human beings feel, that of torture and a diabolically difficult and painful death.

In the worship of Jesus, in the sign of the cross, and in the millennial tears shed over his tragic, agonizing end, the body of God resumed a central place in religious life. "God's body," "God's wounds," and "God's blood" may have been blasphemies, but they were part of folk discourse for centuries, in themselves a kind of backhanded worship. And to the suffering masses of good Christians, nothing was more comforting than the certainty that God Himself for a time had had a human body, had suffered, and had felt physical pain, not just as great as theirs but even greater.

And the Jews—what of them? They went on, you might say, in parallel, except that there were so few that they barely mattered. A boil or a canker sore, some did say, on the great pure body of Christendom. An arrogant, ugly people who persisted in their arcane debates, their absurd abstractions, who refused to understand and believe what everyone knew. A stubborn people who refused to take the wafer and wine in their mouths, who would rather die than follow the only route to salvation, generously offered to them time and time again—believing in and consuming the body and blood of Jesus Christ. All they seemed to be able to do was scoff at true believers and lead the faithful astray, and if they could not see the error of their ways, sooner or later they would have to be gotten rid of.

But if the Jewish god did not have a body, the Jewish people did, and like people throughout the world, they couldn't leave it alone. In fact, they became obsessed with it. They cut a tender part of it off, the seal and symbol of their covenant with their unembodied God. They forged rigorous laws to restrict what was put into their bodies and blessed God in a special prayer over what passed out. Not only their animal sacrifices but the high priests who made them had to be without physical blemish. Indeed in the end you might say that "God's body" did have meaning for the Jews, great meaning: it meant your body, as God wanted it to be.

Their rules about menstrual blood shaped sex roles and rhythms. They declared that a man *owes* a woman sex and mandated its frequency. If very religious, they did not cut the hair at the corners of their beards; Samson, dedicated body and soul to God's will, lost his unique bodily power when his hair was cut off by a woman he had already lost his heart to. "You are dust," the Jews said, "and to dust you will return," so when they at last consigned their bodies to the earth, they placed the least possible barrier between the body and the dust.

But before they discovered God they were a people, defined by blood ties, and their peoplehood, with its mysteries about biological roots, trumped millennial dispersions. Certainly their enemies defined them by blood: corruption, contamination, pollution, or, at a minimum, a taint. In modern times, as they realized that they were subject to certain diseases because of their genes, they began to probe even those tiny builders of the body.

Derided as weak, some Jews absorbed this stereotype, priding themselves only on faith and study. Others in every era bristled against it, building muscle, honing strength and speed, seeking bodily prowess. Some had military exploits to the extent permitted by whatever nation they lived in. In every era, some violent "tough Jews" lived outside the law.

This lasting tension ultimately led to the rebirth of the Jewish nation in Israel, pioneered with contempt for the weakness of Diaspora Jews, and with something resembling a cult of the body, of physical work and self-defense. Today this fault line runs not only between Israelis and Diaspora Jews but within Israel itself, as Jews who fight—religious or not—and Jews who insist on exclusively studying Torah or, today, hew to left-wing sympathies, tug at the country's soul.

But the ultimate definition of the Jewish body has been that of those who hated them. The Nazis had a jingle: "It doesn't matter what the faith, the swinishness is in the race." They defined this swinishness *bodily* and precisely, as German physicians and anthropologists eagerly scientized the identification, deportation, and murder of Jews. In principle every shipment of Jews to the gas chambers had to have a physician's signature, because this was in essence a public health program. German bodies had to be protected from Jewish ones.

2

"The Fruitful Cut"

But by the time the Nazis sought to define them anatomically, Jews had long since taken certain matters into their own hands. For instance, oversized hooked noses had always been a signal feature, and surgical reconstruction had been practiced for half a century—aesthetic surgery that some see as self-hatred or at a minimum a pretense, the act of an impostor, living permanently under a shadow of fear that the genes will out in the faces of the next generation.

We will return to the "Jewish nose," but the first Jewish modification of the body was circumcision, and for most of history it was, for a man, definitive of Jewishness. Today it's a routine operation performed—in the United States at least—on millions of non-Jewish and Jewish babies alike. A shiny ring-shaped clamp is slipped between the head or glans of the penis and the foreskin covering it, down to the ring of raised flesh from which the foreskin springs. The clamp is tightened, cutting off blood supply, and the foreskin is cut away—very carefully—with a scalpel sliding around the ring. Even with a local anesthetic this is a noisy operation; babies don't take kindly to it. Occasionally an infection

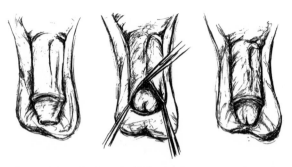

An uncircumsised penis (*left*); the foreskin partly lifted away (*center*); a circumcised penis (*right*).
Original drawing by Sarah Konner, used by permission of the artist.

results, but is almost always treatable. Very, very occasionally—a handful of times out of hundreds of millions—a penis has been lost to complications from such an infection. But a baby is as likely to be killed by a lightning bolt as to suffer such a rare complication, and children also have died from the extra kidney infections that occur in some uncircumcised boys.

Why do it if you're not Jewish? is a question we'll come back to, but for now let's say that it has no definitive general answer. *Why do it if you are?* is something else again, for the seventeenth chapter of Genesis makes it unmistakably clear.[1] "When Abram was ninety years old and nine, the Lord appeared to Abram, and said unto him, 'I am God Almighty; walk before Me, and be thou whole-hearted. And I will make My covenant between Me and thee, and will multiply thee exceedingly' " (vv. 1:2). Sounds pretty good so far. Abram falls on his face and God talks with him further. He mentions the covenant again, changes Abram's name to

Abraham, and says (twice) that Abraham will be "the father of a multitude of nations." And again: " 'I will make thee exceeding fruitful, and I will make nations of thee, and kings shall come out of thee' " (v. 6). God says "covenant" twice more before promising him and his descendants the land of Canaan—Israel—as an everlasting possession.

Could God be softening Abraham up for something with all this largesse? Here is what comes next:

> And as for thee, thou shalt keep My covenant, thou and thy seed after thee throughout their generations. This is My covenant, which ye shall keep, between you and Me and thy seed after thee: every male among you shall be circumcised. And ye shall be circumcised in the flesh of your foreskin; and it shall be a token of a covenant betwixt Me and you. And he that is eight days old shall be circumcised among you, every male throughout your generations . . . and My covenant shall be in your flesh for an everlasting covenant. And the uncircumcised male who is not circumcised in the flesh of his foreskin, that soul shall be cut off from his people, for he hath broken My covenant. (vv. 9–14)

This repetitive litany is as scary as the one just above it is uplifting. *That soul shall be cut off from his people.* Also from his God, of course, but that is not enough. Ostracism was not just psychologically but physically deadly then, yet such is the fate of the man who has not had the sensitive point of his penis sliced off. A multitude of nations Jews may well become, but the Jew who has an intact natural penis between his legs will be a permanent nation of one. And, since circumcision promotes fertility, we can guess that the converse is true—that the natural, unperfected Jewish man will be childless, cut off from his people in future time as well as in present space.

Now if you are male and anything like me, you are already uncomfortable. It's one thing to look down around age ten and figure out that this has been done to you, in some remote past beyond recalling. You imagine yourself a squalling infant who settles down and gets over it. It's quite another to think of yourself as an old man taking a knife to his own member, or as one of his grown sons or servants having it done by the old geezer, who says God told him to do it. Faith would help, no doubt, but even a giant of faith like Abram did not just say *Sure, God, why not?* and start slicing.

According to a midrash—a Rabbinic interpretation or story that grows up around a Bible passage—he approached this new deal with a certain diffidence. So God, according to the midrash, went far beyond the text of Genesis in telling Abraham what was up:

As long as you are uncircumcised, you are imperfect. By performing [circumcision], you will achieve a new degree of holiness and will be elevated above the laws of nature. For twenty generations I have waited for you to come and perform circumcision. If you refuse this *mitzvah*, I shall return the world to nothingness.[2]

Abram still doesn't get the message, and frankly, who can blame him? He challenges God: If the mitzvah, the commandment, is really so great, how come You didn't demand it of Adam? " 'Do not question Me any further,' " God says. " 'You are the one who was found worthy.' " Abram still doesn't like the idea, and his next objection could have come right out of Dale Carnegie. " 'Until now I was able to influence people. Now they will be afraid of approaching me.' " God now gets a little impatient. " 'Do not worry about it. Let it suffice for you that I shall be your God. You will not lose out. By performing the mitzvah . . . you will maintain the existence of the world.' " Even the midrash doesn't record just how reluctantly Abram bent down to take up his knife.

This, like any midrash, is full of Rabbinic insight and religious symbolic echoes. First, God tells Abram he is imperfect. Imperfect? After being created by God in God's own image? Second, God says He has waited twenty generations—the number since Adam—to get this done, and we can ask, with Abram, why the wait? Third, if Abram doesn't step up to the plate, God will uncreate the world. Not, as with Noah, will God merely destroy it, but He will actually reverse the work of Creation. Why the difference? What do these three puzzles mean?

The first was answered many centuries later by the sages of the Kabbalah, the great collection of Jewish mystical writings. God, as they saw it, had deliberately stopped short of completing the work of Creation, leaving not just men but the world itself imperfect, and in countless ways. This was God's strategy for involving human beings in that very work. *Tikkun olam*, it is called—repairing the world. And the

Adam and Eve, now ashamed of their bodies, trying to hide from God. Woodcut illustration by Julius Schnorr von Carolsfeld.

paradigmatic case of *tikkun olam* is circumcision, as if God wanted it clearly known that repairing the world begins not just at home but in your very own, all-too-mortal, frail, physical body. Cut off the cap on the end of your penis and you will get some hint of the price you pay to perfect the world.

God answers the why-the-wait question, but we can expand a bit. Adam wasn't worthy for obvious reasons, which had a lot to do with that same bodily organ. A sinuously phallic little devil led Eve astray, she shared the apple—really an unknown biblical fruit—with Adam (it may have gotten stuck in his throat), and both of them, putting on some of God's own knowledge, had to put on clothing, too, because they became ashamed of their own naked bodies.

Their punishment would be universal and physical: for Eve, pain in childbearing; for Adam, the sweat of his brow in a different kind of labor; and for both, the exchange of pride for shame and of immortality for dust. We are told that Adam soon used his personal organ—unperfected as it was—to seed Eve's first child. He thus became—did God enjoy the irony?—the instrument of God's punishment for Eve: nine months of having a tiny creature rule your body, ending in a world of pain caused by that pregnant coupling. Yet with this same act and organ, they founded the human race.

Abel might have been worthy, but he was too soon cut down by a more typical human. Generations of strange creatures followed. They lived for centuries. "There were giants in the earth in those days," we are told. But every inclination in man's heart "was only evil continually," so God nearly destroyed the world. Noah was worthy of saving because he obeyed seven laws: six "thou shalt nots," against idolatry, blasphemy, murder, sexual crimes (including incest, adultery, bestiality, and sodomy), stealing, and eating a part of a living animal, and one "thou shalt" prescribing courts to ensure obedience to the six "shalt nots."

Noah, too, had a covenant with God, expressed in a sign of exquisite beauty, the rainbow, but it was marked on the airy sky, not the bleeding body; Noah was not considered worthy of circumcision—perhaps because, in a drunken stupor after the flood, he allowed himself to be seen naked by one of his sons (that pesky organ again). In any case, to say that Noah was unworthy of circumcision is simply to say that he could not be the first Jew.

But Abram *was* worthy, and his name and destiny were changed in that momentous act. "Abraham"—"father of multitudes"—became his new path. And by taking that knife to his own body, perfecting it for all future generations, he ensured a transition, too, for his soon-to-be-born people, the ones who had been chosen, who would, by force of the cut, have a special deal with God forever. The word *brit*—in another pronunciation, *bris*—is how the ritual is spoken of, but it doesn't mean "circumcision," it means "covenant." *"My covenant shall be in your flesh."*

Which brings us to God's third puzzling message to Abram. Why uncreate the world? Because this covenant is why God created the world in the first place, and if Abram had drawn back decisively from this precipice, if he had not finally stepped, trustingly, into the covenant, if he had not had the will to cut off that part of his own body—well, then, Creation itself would have been pointless and the world would have disappeared, like a film running very rapidly backward, back to its first, disembodied state, without form, and void.

B ut Abraham did not draw back, and the multitudes he'd been promised issued forth from the organ in question—not slashed in their view, but sculpted, enhanced, completed. There are only a few other uses of the word in the Jewish Bible. Moses is said to have uncircumcised lips, a reference to his speech defect, which God orders him to overcome (*Perfect your speech*, God might have said), so he can face Pharaoh down and lead the Exodus from slavery. A person who defies God's laws is said to have an uncircumcised heart. And an uncircumcised fruit tree bears inedible fruit.

Which may help us solve another mystery: Why should circumcision lead to the birth of multitudes? Because the perfected organ, like the man and the people, are now God's instruments. Howard Eilberg-Schwartz, who studies Jewish law and custom with an anthropologist's eye, calls it "the fruitful cut" because it is inextricably entwined with fertility.[3] And *entwined* turns out to be a fruitful metaphor because circumcision also refers not just to the pruning of juvenile fruit trees but also the grafting of one species on another.

Enemies of the Jews have sometimes claimed that circumcision reflects a negative attitude toward the body and toward sex. But from the outset, Jewish eroticism has been more ambiguous and complex. Adam and Eve become ashamed of their naked bodies, and Eve is condemned to pay for sex with the pain of childbirth. Noah gets drunk and one of his sons sees his nakedness, so this son's son—Canaan—is condemned by Noah himself forever to serve his brothers. But circumcision is about fertility—a more perfect penis is said to make more and better babies. And, to some extent at least, it does protect that organ and its female counterpart from infection.

We now know that circumcised boys are markedly less likely than uncircumcised boys to develop urinary tract infections in infancy and childhood. At first glance this seems to favor a hygienic explanation of the original practice, but there are still two problems. First, until modern times circumcision itself carried a risk of infection, and occasionally a baby boy developed a systemic infection and died. In ancient times the connection between circumcision and these (rare) deaths from bacterial sepsis would probably have been more obvious than any connection between the practice and protection from UTIs. Jewish parents did see this dire consequence, yet those who had lost their sons to it went on to circumcise later sons according to Jewish law.

The other problem is that the elevation in the rate of UTIs in the uncircumcised only brings the boys up to the level of normal girls. True, this is higher than that for circumcised boys, but the argument now seems less compelling. Add to this the fact that careful foreskin hygiene also prevents infections, and the effect doesn't seem to justify the practice. Similarly with the risk of penile cancer in uncircumcised men—good hygiene nullifies the difference.

Studies also show that the wives and other female partners of circumcised men are significantly less likely to get cervical cancer. The vast majority of cervical cancers are caused by the human papillomavirus (HPV), an extremely common sexually transmitted infection. Men with foreskins are more likely to carry HPV. However, here again, proper hygiene is protective. Also, if a relationship is monogamous, the advantage for a woman with a circumcised partner, in terms of protection from cervical cancer, disappears. It is only a significant risk factor if she is having sex with multiple uncircumcised partners or if her one uncircumcised partner is having sex with other women. Circumcision only protects the nonmonogamous.

So the hygiene argument weakens. But why the symbolic connection with fertility? It is useful to look at circumcision in other cultures, and there are many. Muslims circumcise their sons, giving basically the same explanation Jews give: God's covenant with Abraham, which Muslims believe they inherited through Abraham's first son, Ishmael. Traditionally some Islamic communities have performed the rite at puberty or a few years earlier. Modern Muslims do it on the seventh day of life, but consider it permissible to do it at any time during the first few years.

Australian aborigines not only circumcised but in some groups *sub*incised their sons as they entered puberty. Subincision involves slitting the underside of the penis lengthwise from base to tip, in much the way a knife partially splits a sausage; the resulting scar was said to increase a partner's sexual pleasure. In many cultures, circumcision, too, was done at puberty. Among the Ngatatjara of the Gibson Desert, the boy was laid across the backs of a row of friends on their hands and knees, making a living table, and the foreskin was cut off with a stone blade. All this took place in the dramatic setting of a dance—dedicated to the Kangaroo, a sacred animal—around a huge bonfire. Like many puberty rituals, it was a test of the boy's willingness to suffer pain calmly; it proved he was now a man.

For the Thonga of South Africa, the operation was central to a months-long pubertal initiation rite. A group of boys ran a gauntlet between two rows of grown men who stripped them, cut off their hair, and beat them with clubs. Then, intimidating men draped in lions' manes confronted them. Made to sit on a rock, each boy was hit from behind, turned reflexively, and had his foreskin seized and cut off in two deft strokes by one of the "lion men." The boys spent three months recovering, naked except for leaves on the wound, while having drummed into them the secrets and, more important, the identity of manhood. If a woman so much as gazed on their genital garlands during this time, she was supposed to have been killed.

Farther north, the Ndembu of Zambia circumcised their boys earlier, between ages eight and ten, accompanied by a ritual dance that imitated lions. Here, too, the circumciser was said to be lionlike, and his job was to cut the boy's tie to his mother. The boys were dramatically painted with white clay and became men through a months-long ritual time of healing and teaching. The Merina of Madagascar did it much earlier, when boys were a year or two old. Relatives assembled for a quiet, dignified ritual that emphasized continuity with the ancestors, and it ensured the little boy ultimate potency and fertility.

This theme of fertility is often explicit. In many cultures it was a pubertal rite of passage, a gateway to manhood. African circumcision rites in particular often make potency and fertility symbolism explicit. Dances attending circumcision may mimic copulation. Medicine made from the hard wood of fruit trees was applied to the wound, to evoke the hardness and fruitfulness of a penis. This symbolic wound

Brit Milah (Covenant of Circumcision) as depicted in
the 1707 edition of *Minhagim* (Customs), published by
Solomon ben Joseph Proops, Amsterdam.

helps change a boy into a man—hard, potent, fertile, resistant to pain, cut from the softness of mother love and linked to his male ancestors by an endless chain of repetitions of this rite, which in each new generation makes boys more not just physically but in every important way like their fathers.

Since Jews do it at eight days, not at puberty, the transformation from boy to man is not part of the meaning. Yet the Torah does emphasize fertility: Just before giving the order to Abram, God says, "I will make thee exceeding fruitful, and I will make nations of thee, and kings shall come out of thee" (Gen. 17:6). God changes his name to Abraham, implying fatherhood, and announces both the covenant and its very physical symbol. Now, for the first time, his body is completely God's body. Through both Ishmael and Isaac, Abraham becomes the most famously potent man in the Western tradition.

All Jewish circumcisions since Abraham's symbolize the continuity of the male line, but his did the opposite: It *broke* his ties to his fathers, idolaters one and all. He will have uncountable descendants, but only by denying his ancestors. Yet for all subsequent generations, the symbolic wound of circumcision will confirm the lineage of all Jews back to Abraham. Converts, who also must be circumcised, are squarely in this line; *this* bodily inheritance is culturally transmitted. And God's dreadful words—"that soul shall be cut off from his people"—mean not just ostracism but sterility, the opposite of God's promise to Abraham. The childless, uncircumcised man is cut off not just from the past and present but from the future of his people.

Secular Bible scholarship has for more than a century tried to work out the separate human authorship of the text and concludes that the circumcision part of Genesis was composed by the Priestly author—probably much later than the rest of the book, in First Temple times. However old circumcision was, the Israelite priesthood wanted to reconfirm its importance and make its meaning clear. It could not be a pagan fertility rite but the mark of a covenant with the one true God, who assures descendants for his people and commands them to make the fruitful cut, transforming the bodies of Jewish men forever.

We may never know for certain why the Jews, from such an ancient time, circumcised their sons. We do know the explanations they gave and how seriously they took it: throughout not merely centuries but millennia, Jews have risked their lives and the lives of their sons to keep this practice. Greek tyrants in the time of the Maccabees punished it by death and threw Jewish mothers off cliffs with their just-circumcised sons dangling from ropes around their necks. German tyrants in our own time used circumcision to separate Jewish men and boys from others and send them to be murdered. Yet in both these times and in all times before and since, Jews blessed God, formally acknowledging the covenant with Abraham, and circumcised the next baby boy, and the next. Spinoza, apostate though he was, believed that "it alone would preserve the nation forever." Unquestionably it is the first and the most important defining and self-defining feature of the Jewish body.[4]

3

Greeks and Jews

While the Jews were defining—some would say marring—their bodies, other people were defining theirs. Camille Paglia, a brilliant scholar and culture critic, has said that the Jewish God made man in His image, but the Greeks made their gods in man's. "The Greek gods have a higher human beauty, their flesh incorruptible yet sensual."[1] Among the greatest of Greek arts were sculpture and painting, forbidden to Jews, and they used these arts to depict the gorgeous and vivid bodies of gods, but also of women and men.

In many if not most cases, these depictions were nude and were meant to be perfect. The Greeks had contempt for bodily deformity and mutilation of any kind, even among the gods. Hephaestus (the Roman Vulcan) is a cripple married to Aphrodite, that queen of sexuality and beauty, but he is cuckolded and a laughingstock among the gods.

In addition to coaxing idealized bodies out of stone, the Greeks sculpted their own living bodies with equal artistry and care. While the defeated Jews were in exile in Babylon, becoming obsessed with texts about their abstract God, the

Greeks held athletic events where all contestants were naked. These young men were as beautiful as statues, carved through obsessive exercise and practice, and all observers expected to see them in the flesh, pushing the outer boundaries of sprinting, leaping, wrestling, throwing—whatever the human body can do.

By the time Alexander the Great swept over the East in 332 BCE, and incidentally over the Jews, they were already the "philosophers by race" that Aristotle's student Theophrastus made them out to be. Three serious rebellions—one against the Greeks, temporarily successful, and two against the Romans, catastrophic failures—would demonstrate that the Jews were not prepared to rely exclusively on philosophy or even religion. They, too, had soldierly skills, physical courage, and a will to fight. What Alexander brought from Greece became what we call Hellenism only through the absorption of elements from conquered cultures, but it has long been known that the Greeks influenced the Jews in philosophy, literature, and custom.

Yet despite all these common features and currents of mutual influence, there is much truth in the contrast between the Hellenic or Greco-Roman culture and the Hebraic or Jewish one. This contrast became a theme of nineteenth-century philosophy and literary criticism, and has probably been at times exaggerated.

But consider. The Greeks built philosophic systems to understand the universe, while the Jews proclaimed divinely inspired ethical law. The Greeks blazed paths in geometry and engineering to master the physical world, but in that sphere the Jews could only try to master the Greeks' discoveries. Aristotle systematized all human knowledge, while Jewish prophets in mystical visions railed against idolatry and selfishness. The Greeks created still unsurpassed works of sculpture and drama and poetry, while the Jews were prohibited plastic arts and disdained drama, but crafted one of the world's first and greatest ethical literatures.

Recent scholarship has made much of the mutual influence, and some scholars reject the old Hellenism-Judaism contrasts.[2] This certainly applies to the realm of philosophy, and Talmudic styles of argument were influenced by Greek traditions. The Passover seder is in some ways a symposium, and the word for the piece of matzah children search for at the seder's end—*afikomen*—comes from the Greek word for after-dinner entertainment. Jews throughout the growing Diaspora spoke Greek and carved their names in Greek letters next to Jewish symbols on their tombstones. Jewish "Hellenizers" were so numerous as to foreshadow the modern Jewish-American tide of assimilation; many tried to be Greek in every way.

But for the Jews who wanted to stay Jewish—in Israel, Egypt, and elsewhere—cultural conflict led to four major rebellions. For those who stubbornly believed in the Jewish religion, the marriage between Greco-Roman and Jewish culture foundered on two questions: *Does God have a body?* and *How do human bodies become godly?* To each, the two cultures gave starkly different answers. We have already seen the cost in blood and destruction that resulted from different answers to the first question; the Jewish answer to the second was circumcision (abhorrent to Greco-Roman views), laws of dietary and menstrual purity, and a list of formulaic daily blessings. For the Greeks and Romans, making the body godly meant toning it in gymnasiums for athletic events honoring the gods.

Athleticism was more than sport—it was central to the realization of *arête*, or virtue. The original Olympic games were only the most important of the frequent competitions throughout Greece. These festivals were open to all freeborn young men from wealthy families, and their training began at around age twelve. And the "all" in that sentence is serious; Hellenism was a universal culture, possibly the first. The Greeks and Romans extended their empires so successfully because their most important paths to achievement were open; in any culture Hellenism tried to absorb, all freeborn wealthy men might apply.

But what of the Jews? While Jewish boys were preparing for their religious coming-of-age, Greek boys (and all non-Greeks who aspired to be Hellenic) studied philosophy, music, and the arts, but their training always included wrestling schools and gymnasiums as well. Women were strictly prohibited. Each boy had an adult male mentor, but the older man was clothed and bearded while the younger was smooth-faced and naked. Indeed, the word *gymnasium* comes from *gymnos*, the word for "naked." In these settings young men were not only honed for competition and combat but groomed for their civic duties and the privileges of wealth and class. The older men acted as teachers, coaches, referees, and mentors, as in the old all-male American private (or English "public") schools.

Greek gymnasium mentors might take a sexual interest in the boys, and this was considered legitimate, although abstinence was preferable for athletes. Plato's *Symposium* shows that many Greek men considered relationships with boys to be the highest form of love. Erotic relations aside, gymnasiums and baths were bastions of male power where men and boys socialized, bonded, and planned for the future. Much of political and social importance came out of conversations among men who were mostly naked. And all competitions were held in the nude, because the body's beauty was being celebrated and because nudity showed that all young men were equal in the eyes of the gods.

Only winning mattered and the humiliated losers—including those who today would win silver or bronze—went home in disgrace. The winner was thought to be favored by the gods, and so victory meant not just training and prowess but *arête*—virtue itself. Everyone wanted to bask in the reflected glory of that godlike (and god-loved) young man, naked except for the winner's laurel wreath. The greatest athletes became demigods, like the men of myth whose parents were one human and one god.

Needless to say, Jewish boys and men had a few problems. First and foremost, however wealthy, fashionable, assimilated, and articulate in Greek they and their families might be, if they were circumcised they were mutilated; their bodies might be perfect in the Jewish sense but could never be so in the Greek sense, however athletically gifted they were, however hard they trained. They could not win because they could not compete; they would be laughed or driven out of the gymnasium.

There is no more striking way to demonstrate the depth of this divide and the desire of many Jews to cross it than to consider this fact: Many Jewish men had their circumcisions surgically reversed.[3] Epispasm, decircumcision, or uncircumcision, as the procedure is called, was alluded to as early as the first book of Maccabees, when "some of the people eagerly went to the king, who authorized them to observe the ordinances of the Gentiles. So they built a gymnasium in Jerusalem, according to Gentile custom, and removed the marks of circumcision and abandoned the holy covenant" (1:12–15). The Roman physician Celsus described two surgical techniques in his *De medicina libri octo*, redescribed with little change by Galen. These and other procedures were used throughout European history and, not surprisingly, became more common in German-occupied Europe.

But it was not just because of this obstacle that Jewish and Greco-Roman culture diverged, especially after the two unsuccessful rebellions against Roman rule in Israel and the spread of Rabbinic Judaism throughout the expanding Diaspora. The two cultures now had dramatically different ideas about the good life, and for Jews the good life was the religious life of the mind. This is not to disparage the genius of Greco-Roman arts and sciences or even the cult of the body as one way of keeping the mind sound and healthy. But for ordinary Jews the body, while sacred, and always the object of religious regulation, was not to be a focus of personal enhancement. Meanwhile, the more or less relentless military exploits of the European ruling classes ensured that athletic prowess would be associated with virtue for many centuries, from the gymnasiums of Athens to the playing fields of Eton and Harrow.

So the enduring contrast was in the clash of bodies. Greeks won wars, Jews usually lost them. Greeks had gorgeous embodied gods, Jews had one dimly imagined unembodied God. Greeks indulged in almost unrestrained feasts, while Jews seemed to delight in dietary restrictions. Greeks swore oaths over slices of wild boar; Jews, as the Roman satirist Juvenal later put it, suffered pigs to attain old age. Greeks had naked athletic competitions, Jews had intense but decorous theological disputations. Greeks had public baths where sybaritic men met beautiful boys and all could display their carefully kept, finely crafted bodies; Jews had ritual baths in which solitary sinners could be purified, one by one. The Greeks considered links between men the highest form of love; the Jews saw homosexual love as a heinous sin.

To be sure, not all the Greeks believed in their gods, and the more sophisticated among them met the most educated, secular Jews on common philosophical ground. Despite some disagreements, Aristotle's disciples and the Greco-Roman-Jewish philosopher Philo understood each other. But Philos were few and far between, and the Jews did not fight war after war against Greek and Roman rule because there were no differences that mattered. There were many similarities between Greco-Roman and Jewish culture, but there were differences to die for.

To really grasp the difference between Jewish and Greco-Roman (read: *European*) views of the body, we have to distinguish two very different Greek traditions, the Apollonian and the Dionysian. So far we have talked mainly about the Apollonian: a cult of the body, but an austere one. The god Apollo, the victor in the first Olympic games, is a young man—an ephebe—in Greek depictions, and he shares the beauty of young gymnasium athletes. But his is a nonsexual, distant sort of beauty. Sex might link mentor and ephebe, but not because the young man experienced the desire; rather, his very purity made him the highest object of mature male lust. Apollo's relations with women are mostly brief conquests and he is the god of athletes because his path strengthens and purifies the body. His twin sister Artemis (Diana) is both hunter and runner; her cool, near-boyish beauty makes her his ideal counterpart.

Dionysus—Bacchus—on the other hand, is the god of wine and drunkenness, and this makes him both a comforter of suffering humanity and an instigator of sometimes terrible ecstasy. He gives us the word *bacchanalia*, the name of his festival, but also, according to the *American Heritage Dictionary*, "a riotous, boisterous, or drunken festivity; a revel." Most instructive about him perhaps is Euripides' play *The Bacchae*, the tale of how Dionysus came to Greece. It tells of Theban women seized by the god's ecstasy with tragic effect; one of them, a member of the royal family, blindly kills her son, who has dared to doubt the god's immortal status. She and the other women literally tear the boy—who you might say has the youth, pride, skill, and beauty of Apollo—limb from limb, and so Dionysus drags the Theban royal house down to its doom.

Much of what we know about Dionysus and his role in Greek culture comes from this play.[4] The chorus of his devotees describes him "sweet upon the mountains" but also says "He hunts the wild goat and kills it / He delights in the raw flesh," while the earth flows with milk, wine, and bees' nectar. He is savage, yet seductive. He gives "the gladness of the grape" to rich and poor alike, blesses the flute with laughter and us with "the loosing of cares." Without him there would be "no love, no Aphrodite either, nor other pleasure left to men." He "loves the goddess Peace . . . preserver of the young" but, like Jehovah, he is a jealous god and takes revenge on scoffers.

No wine, no love, no Aphrodite? That means no sex and no fertility as well. Apollo's lust is cold, but the lust inspired by Dionysus is steeped in comforting wine and laced with ecstasy. Aphrodite (Venus) goes as well with Dionysus as Artemis with Apollo. Wine and desire bring a sorely needed Dionysian wildness to our too-well-governed Appolonian human lives.

The philosopher Friedrich Nietzsche, the anthropologist Ruth Benedict, and many others have made much of the Apollonian-Dionysian distinction. Camille Paglia writes:

> The quarrel between Apollo and Dionysus is the quarrel between the higher cortex and the older limbic and

reptilian brains. . . . Dionysus is energy unbound, mad, callous, destructive, wasteful. Apollo is law, history, tradition, the dignity and safety of custom and form. . . . [Dionysus] is the god of theater, masked balls, and free love—but also of anarchy, gang rape, and mass murder. . . . Frosty Apollo has a sculptural coherence and clarity. The Apollonian . . . strict, rigid, and contained, is western personality as work of art, haughty and elegant. . . . Dreams are Dionysian magic in the sensory inflammation of sleep. . . . Apollo binds together and battens down against the storm of nature.[5]

But which *really* reflects the Greco-Roman worldview? Both, and that is the beauty of polytheistic belief. You don't have to choose one path or the other, because different paths are dear to different gods. Human personalities may naturally lean one way or another, but ideally we should not go to extremes, since satisfying one god could conceivably anger another. Euripides' play, which dramatizes the entrance of Dionysus onto the sacred stage of Greece, shows how a pantheon of varied gods can make room for another—in this case as in many, a god dear to another people, influencing the Hellenes as they themselves Hellenize others.

My grandparents, if told about Apollo and Dionysus, would probably just have said, *Dos is nit Yiddish!* (This is not Jewish!) or maybe even *Dionysus, shmionysus.* But *how* is it not Jewish, or even Hebraic? First, of course, even two gods are one too many, an affront to the second commandment. Up to

וَאֶשְׂמַח בְּשִׂמְחַת תּוֹרַת

Revels at *Simchat Torah* (The Rejoicing of the Law), as
shown on a *Simchat Torah* flag. This is one of the two
times a year when Jews get a bit Dionysian (the other
is Purim), but just the wine and dancing, not the
sex or violence. Mostly, they are high on Torah.
Women are not included.
Israel Museum, used by permission.

a point, the Jewish God contains within one being the entire
range of inclinations in the pantheon. Talmudic Judaism was
content to leave this claim as an abstraction, but the later
rabbis of the Kabbalah not only listed thirteen different
attributes of God, they even gave God a symbolic humanlike
body, locating the attributes in different body parts. Nevertheless, this bit of backsliding was metaphoric, and in any
case it still depicted one God with one "body" and had limited influence.

Second, Apollo and Dionysus do not just represent different qualities, they embody them, specifically, with implica-

tions for human behavior. Apollo keeps his sacred body in trim shape and is not only beautiful but also victorious in games; these physical qualities enable him to bed numerous women, divine and human, but in an almost sexless sort of way. Artemis, his twin, is chaste; she must avoid sex to be mistress of the hunt, and even men are urged to keep sex away from athletic preparation and competition. Dionysus, for his part, revels with the revelers, relishing drunken wildness and the sex that often follows. Aphrodite's beauty is dazzling, erotic, and fertile. She reaches far beneath a man's aesthetic wonder to his well of driven, helpless, and dangerous sexuality. Throughout the Greco-Roman world in time and space, the greatest artists created representations of the bodies of these gods—especially Apollo and Aphrodite, which both served and sacralized the natural human desire to gaze upon physical beauty. The second commandment, "Thou shalt not make unto thee any graven images," ensured that Jews would recoil from any such thing.

Finally, the implications of these gods for human action—their moral consequences—were also not Jewish. Neither Apollo's stringently athletic and homoerotic games nor the orgiastic ecstasies of the feasts of Dionysus had any place in the Hebraic or Jewish worldview. Physical health and strength were valued, to be sure, and, in Temple times, were necessary for war, but the body beautiful, chaste or not, was not the path to God. Wine was nice, but more for ritual purposes than comfort or, certainly, ecstasy. It was shared by bride and groom in the wedding ceremony, and the breaking of the glass, sometimes followed by ribald jokes, had sexual connotations whatever its other meanings. This echoed an earlier time when a glass of red wine was cast against a white wall and, farther back, a time when the display of a blood-stained white sheet at once proved both the virginity of the bride and the virility of the groom.[6]

You could get drunk twice a year, on festivals meant for religious rejoicing. The ritually prescribed four cups of wine at the Passover seder were meant to help you relax—to show that, like the Greeks and Romans, you were free. As for sex, a bacchanalia would have been for Jews not sacred but sacrilege. And although sex was not just for procreation, its only other purpose was to create and, again and again, renew the bond between a loving husband and wife. Jews often fell short of these ideals, but they were not the ideals of Greece and Rome.

Although Christianity (in theory) set the Dionysian aside, the Apollonian became and remains the ideal of the ruling classes of Europe. As the Jews were an extension of ancient Rabbinic Judaism, the Christians became the heirs of Apollonian Greece and Rome. We will revisit this parallel progress, but Christians excluded Jews from both the playing fields and the battlefields until these separate streams met again in the nineteenth century. Yet the Dionysian in us does not stay suppressed forever, and so there have been periodic outbursts of the dark side of mind and body throughout European history, often produced by and masquerading as Apollonian Christianity; for the Jews, these flashes of Dionysian rage could only end in tears.

4

Adam's Rib?

Dionysus and his festivals aside, great rabbis do have great sexual appetites, as we have seen, and therefore (not being ecstatic Greeks) must have great strength of will to bring them under control. The bawdy aspect of the Talmud is nowhere highlighted more forcefully than in the section discussing Rabbi Yishmael's and Rabbi Yose's bodies.[1] When they "happened to meet each other, a pair of oxen could pass between them and not touch them," a way of describing their superhuman girth when standing gut to gut. A Roman matron says, "Your children are not yours!" Those who know interpret this as a sexual taunt at their obesity; she means they were too fat to have sex.

The Talmud records two traditions about their replies: "There are some who say that they said to her thus: 'For as a man is, so is his strength,' " a verse from Judges (8 21). By this, scholars say, they meant they had the sexual organs and prowess to bridge the gap. But, "There are others who say that they answered her as follows: 'Love presses the flesh.' "

Indeed, or the world would long since be bereft of chubby people. But there is more: "Rabbi Yohanan said: The limb of

Rabbi Yishmael . . . was like a water-skin measuring nine *kavs*. Rav Pappa said: Rabbi Yohanan's limb was like a water-skin measuring five *kavs*. And some say: Measuring three *kavs*. That of Rav Pappa himself was like the baskets of Harpanya."

In some interpretations, "limb" means belly, but others use the translation "member" and understand the Hebrew word to mean "genitals." The great Rabbi Solomon Luria of the sixteenth century held that these Herculean appendages were reflections of the sages' sexual passions, and therefore, again, of their self-control. And immediately after this braggadocio about mammoth members, as if to deflect any possible talk of the grotesque, Rabbi Yohanan begins touting his own physical beauty, introducing a long discussion of just how gorgeous the sages were.

Perhaps because of the price paid in circumcision, perhaps because of "be fruitful and multiply" (the first commandment in the Bible), perhaps because, as God said before making Eve, "it is not good for the man to be alone," or perhaps only because a penis perfected by circumcision ought to be used for *something*, celibacy has never been valued by Jews. Temporary abstinence, sure; rules hemming you in from every direction of the compass, yes; temperance, absolutely; but actually trying *never* to have sex—even with another person? a human? of different gender? whom you're married to? *You have to be kidding*—the Talmud seems to say, as strongly as Philip Roth might. It's a mitzvah—meaning both a commandment and a good deed. Yet sex is very dangerous; it brings unwanted people into the world, wrecks reputations, breaks up families, and subjugates both genders from within (mostly men) and without (mostly women). So *get* it, yes, but for God's sake, *get it under control.*

But how?

Well, you don't do it outside of marriage, with a child or a relative, by yourself, with a same-sex partner, or during menstruation, but that's just for starters. The Talmud doesn't just say, *Only within marriage.* It says that you must be in the right frame of mind when you have sex, or it's not the kind of sex that is permitted and encouraged. Unlike some other religious traditions, the purpose of Jewish sex is not just to make babies; ultimately that is the central purpose, but a nearly equally important purpose is to strengthen the marital bond, without which the family—the intimate environment vital to children as well as husband and wife—will fail.

The Torah (Exod. 21 10) says, "He may not diminish her allowance, clothing, or conjugal rights," and these three husbandly obligations are spelled out in every traditional Jewish marriage contract. One way "conjugal rights" are viewed is in terms of simple frequency. But the Ramban, one of the greatest of medieval rabbis, interprets the term differently. "Diminish," to him, is not numerical but spiritual: "Her physical intimacy, the cover of her bed, and her time of love he may not withhold from her. . . . The reason is to ensure that he will not lie with her as if by chance and on the ground, as one has intercourse with a prostitute, whereas another wife reposes in a bed of honor where husband and wife are 'as one flesh.' "[2]

The last phrase is from Genesis, and they are one flesh from the moment Eve is created to ease Adam's loneliness. In the version in which she is made from one of his ribs, He says, "This is now bone of My bones and flesh of My flesh. . . . Therefore shall a man leave his father and his mother and cling to his wife" (Gen. 2 23). *One flesh*, given the intertwining of body and soul, also means one soul. And every sexual act should make that unity more real.

One way to understand how Judaism views sex is to look at the list of nine ways that the wrong frame of mind can (according to the Rabbis) hurt the child that emerges from the act; unfairly no doubt, but pointedly not just the sins but the very mood of the father or mother *in that moment* may haunt the resulting children. Superstition, perhaps, quite unfair but very revealing of the beliefs of religious Jews about sex. First, there can be no force, a devastating violation of intimacy. Second, the man must not hate his wife. Third, neither partner must be in mourning, when they will lack the mental energy needed to enhance union. Fourth, it cannot be the result of a deal—you do this for me and I'll do something else for you—for this, the Rabbis say, can only drive a couple apart. Fifth, if sex occurs in the middle of a quarrel, the union is blemished, even in the absence of general hatred; Ravad said, "This is like illicit prostitution, since it is not amidst love."[3]

Sixth, neither partner may be drunk, because a drunken person cannot concentrate on the lover nor on the act of consecration. (So much for Dionysus.) Sex with someone who is asleep is similar, while daytime sex is considered praiseworthy. Seventh, a man may not have sex with his wife if he is intending to divorce her. Eighth, a man must not be involved with nor have his mind on another woman. And ninth and finally, the sexual act must not result from a coarse or brazen overture, but from tenderness, respect, and love. Thus, the nine commandments of coupling.

In sum—despite the glass-breaking jokes at weddings—you don't fuck, you quite literally make love. It is vital to understand how seriously these warnings were meant to be taken; nothing in Jewish life is more important than a child, yet the child could be damaged if the wrong kind of intercourse led to that child's birth. Rashi, the great medieval commentator on the Torah and the Talmud, distinguished between "complete" intercourse and "plain" or "illicit" intercourse. Complete intercourse serves and mends the bond between the lovers; plain or illicit intercourse is sex for its own sake and not the Jewish way.[4]

Needless to say, even for a people who more or less accepted it, sex had a down side. Just as the Bible is charged with sexual themes, so has Jewish folklore been, right back to the beginning. And, as in the Bible, much of the sex has negative consequences, "Be fruitful and multiply" notwithstanding. Take Lilith, a woman whose history goes back almost before the Bible begins. The Torah gives two different versions of how men and women came to be. In one, God puts Adam to sleep and makes him a helpmeet from one of his ribs, but in the other, earlier version the two sexes are invented simultaneously: "Male and female created He them."

According to Jewish legend,[5] Eve was not the woman created simultaneously with Adam in this account, Lilith was, and the problem with Lilith was precisely that she was on equal terms with Adam from the start. She refused to be ruled by him, and to make matters worse, she insisted that she be on top when they had sex. Ancient Israel being a patriarchal culture, this kind of woman could hardly be allowed to be the mother of all humankind. So God made a new woman from Adam's rib. But alas, this second draft didn't quite know her place either, and there was an incident with a snake regarding an apple, with permanent sexual repercussions.

But God in His wisdom did not destroy Lilith; he condemned her to the other world, where she found remarkable powers. Equal to any man yet scorned by God, she became the bane of men's existence, tormenting them throughout eternity—especially the ones who would devote themselves to God. Did a man's thoughts turn to lust in bed at night—and not lust for his wife? Did he get an involuntary erection? Did he even, God forbid, have a wet dream? The folk explanation was straightforward: Lilith had paid him a visit, searching for semen. Every wet dream, or worse, masturbatory episode might make Lilith pregnant and generate more of her uncountable demons.

Lilith is always ready to lead a man astray, whether he is asleep in bed or awake and out and about:

> She dresses herself in finery like an abominable harlot and stands at the corners of streets and highways in order to attract men. When a fool approaches her, she embraces him and kisses him, and mixes her wine lees with snake poison for him. Once he has drunk, he turns aside after her. . . .
>
> [This] is the finery that she uses to seduce mankind: her hair is long, red like a lily; her face is white and pink; six pendants hang at her ears . . . all the ornaments of the East encircle her neck; her mouth is shaped like a tiny door, beautified with cosmetic; her tongue is sharp like a sword; her words smooth as oil; her lips beautiful, red as a lily, sweetened with all the sweetnesses in the world; she is dressed in purple, and attired with thirty-nine items of finery.[6]

Delilah on speed; but even Samson's fate was enviable compared with that of the man who dallies with Lilith:

> This fool turns after her, and drinks from the cup of wine, and commits harlotry with her, completely enamored of her. What does she do? She leaves him asleep on the bed and ascends to the realms above, accuses him, obtains authority, and descends. The fool wakes up, thinking to sport with her as before, but she takes off her finery, and turns into a fierce warrior, facing him in a garment of flaming fire, a vision of dread, terrifying both body and soul, full of horrific eyes, a sharpened

Amulet to protect a newborn from Lilith. Persia, eighteenth century. Lilith's arms are outstretched but
bound. "Protect this newborn child from all harm" is
inscribed on her body. The names of Adam, Eve, the
patriarchs, and the matriarchs appear on either side of
the figure. Above it appear the first few words of the
Priestly Blessing (Numbers 6:22–27), recited by parents
over children. Below it, the beginning of Psalm 121, "I
will lift up mine eyes unto the hills . . ."
From Lilith: The First Eve, *by S. Hurwitz. Used by permission of
Daimon Verlag, Einsiedeln, Switzerland.*

sword in his hand with drops of poison suspended from
it. He kills the fool, and throws him into Gehinnom.[7]

Gehinnom is hell, the fire that burns forever. In this terrifying legend, the delicious seductress changes into one of
God's (or Satan's?) warriors. In a Greek myth, perhaps, the
sinner would have fought back. But this is no case of Jacob
wrestling the angel, more like Yankl wrestling the devil, and
his Jewish body proves weak in more ways than one.

Not all demons come from hapless men's solitary nocturnal passions. Some were created by God, who didn't have time to add their bodies before the first Sabbath eve fell, so they ended up as bodiless wandering souls.[8] Some came from wicked people who had died. Still others arose from Adam's dalliances with she-devils after he and his wayward bride were forced out of Eden. But Lilith and her impish legion tempt men relentlessly, which is why men must be married, faithful, and have sex as often as possible with their wives.

At least since Second Temple times, those wives were supposed to be Jewish. But Jewish men are not only tempted by Lilith, queen of solitary sex, they are tempted by the shiksa—the Gentile woman—famously lying in wait with almost Lilith-like temptations to draw the nice Jewish boy away from his duties and his people. *Shiksa* was originally and sometimes still is very derogatory; it is the feminine version of a Yiddishized Hebrew word, *sheketz*, meaning "blemished" or "loathed." But a century of use by American Jewish writers and comedians has given it a more benign, even complimentary meaning, as in Philip Roth's *Portnoy's Complaint*, for instance, or the Seinfeld episode in which several Jewish men are drawn to the same woman's "shiks-appeal." In many similar contexts, the word implies something desirable and (for a Jewish man) almost unattainable in a woman, whom we might now call the shiksa-Goddess—tall, slim, but well built, with a strapping sort of health, blue-eyed, and blond. Even when the last two characteristics were missing, the shape of the face—high, well-defined cheekbones, big eyes, a childlike jaw, and, of course, a small, straight nose—conformed to the classic Northern European type.

Jewish women who have been famous for their beauty—like Sarah Bernhardt, a goddess of the nineteenth-century European stage; Theda Bara, the matinee idol of silent film (whose real name was Theodosia Burr Goodman); or Lauren Bacall, the 1940s movie star and partner of Humphrey Bogart on and off the silver screen (who started life as Betty Perske)—have neither "looked Jewish" as defined by the larger culture nor publicly identified as Jews in any significant way. The same applies to more recent examples, like actresses Gwyneth Paltrow (descended from a family of famous rabbis named Paltrowitz), Winona Ryder (née Winona Laura Horowitz), and Rachel Weisz, whose parents are Holocaust survivors. Given the face they show to the world, in a sense these women are *Jewish* shiksa-goddesses.

The lure of the non-Jewish woman begins in the Bible, and it isn't at first considered at all bad. The sons of Jacob captured foreign wives by force, and the Tribes of Israel were born. Joseph married the daughter of an Egyptian priest, yet their sons' names are invoked by Jews every Friday night in blessing their own sons. Moses took Zipporah, the daughter of a priest of Midian, and went on to be God's greatest messenger. Boaz wed Ruth, a Moabite woman who became the ancestor of King David and of the Messiah. Samson's shiksa-hunger did not turn out so well, and Delilah is far more emblematic than Zipporah or Ruth of the role of the Gentile woman later in Jewish history. Like Lilith, she is wonderfully appealing on the outside, but *sheketz*—an object of loathing—on the inside.

Moses notwithstanding, in the Torah itself God forbids intermarriage with seven specific peoples, including the Hittites and the Canaanites, saying that it will make the Hebrews turn away from the God of Israel and serve other gods. (The same section of Deuteronomy commands the Hebrews to destroy these peoples' altars and burn their graven images.) Ezra, returning to Israel after the Babylonian exile, finds so many intermarried couples that he is moved to dissolve these unions and forbid them thereafter. He even sends the non-Jewish wives and children away, which seems odd given that in ancient Israel, Jewishness descended through the father.

Today, theoretically, Judaism treats converts the same way it treats born Jews, or better, since they are "Jews by Choice," and conversion before marriage resolves some of these contradictions. But this doesn't change the fact that desire for the stranger is a motivating factor in such marriages. Conversion or not, the genetic evidence clearly shows that the Jews imported genes from whatever non-Jewish population they lived among, in one phase or another of their history, and you don't import (or export) genes without an attraction toward the one who is different. Even in cases of rape or concubine-capture, someone has to desire the forbidden, mysterious other.

In all the places where they lived as outsiders, *different* usually meant "better than Jews," at least in the eyes of the dominant people. So those Jews who had a sense of inferiority and wanted to overcome it might feel drawn to members of the opposite sex who belonged to that better class of prospects. Usually they could not have acted on this impulse, but when did that ever shut down desire? It is always the dominant people who define what is beautiful. So even the ghetto-bound, downtrodden Jewish "Other" would get a glimpse of the mainstream upper crust decked out in all its finery, and see statues and pictures and, later, photos and plays and movies, and they would have their erotic taste strongly shaped by non-Jews.

The ultimate realization of this is the Jewish weakness for blondes. Of course, this is not just Jewish—it's African American, Mediterranean, Asian, Middle Eastern. Any kind of minority status that includes being darker, whether in hair, eyes, or skin, often results in a hunger, in men at least (and it's men who do most of the hungering), for this unattainable, godlike, "superior" kind of partner. The unconscious idea seems to be that some of the status of the blonde will rub off on the Jew or the black, or, for men, the conquest of such a prize (consider "trophy wives") would prove that they are not after all inferior. Marriage, romance, and sex are the ultimate signs of acceptance; they take away the stigma of being outside looking in, and if children result from the union, this effect should be greater for them. Add to all this the fact that the Other is almost always considered hypersexual—this superstition works both ways—and also the fact that difference alone can be an aphrodisiac, and you have a recipe for a special type of longing.

It may be superficial at the outset, but it doesn't have to

King David spies on Bathsheba as she bathes. Her beauty
leads him to his greatest sin, as well as to the birth of
Solomon. Woodcut illustration by Julius Schnorr
von Carolsfeld.

end that way—looks can lead to love, whether or not ethnic
boundaries are crossed. Even the Jewish women considered
beautiful have been taller, slimmer, and fairer than average.
Abraham's love for Sarah, Jacob's for Rachel, David's for
Bathsheba, Boaz's for Ruth, and even a Persian tyrant's for
the simply lovely Esther had much in common with the ordinary male penchant for beauty. In all these matches it played
a role, and in the last two, difference did as well—with fine
results. We are certainly told that these women were beautiful and also that *that* mattered to these exceptional men. We
don't have to act on impulse, but we can't really control our
inner response to beauty, however superficial that response
may seem, even to ourselves.

5

Dangerous Bodies

The attractiveness in so many ethnic groups of ever-paler skin or hair is also about whiteness, and whiteness is very often about purity. Most people in the world are not white and never have been, and whatever chances of history led Northern Europe and Britain to dominate the planet in the past few centuries strengthened the identification of whiteness with goodness. But purity itself can just as well be black as white, and this is one of many dichotomies that countless cultures, perhaps all, have imposed on a real world of continuous shades of gray.

This dichotomizing tendency takes advantage of a natural weakness of the human mind: intolerance for ambiguity. We don't like the grays; we prefer contrasts that are "like night and day": us and them, civilization and barbarism, Jew and Gentile, Christian and heathen, tame and wild, village and wilderness, clean and dirty, chaste and defiled, black and white, and of course, good and evil. This tragic distorting tendency underlies all racism, chauvinism, and religious war. Our primitive and enduring reaction to blurred boundaries is that they risk pollution, and our minds prefer the comfort of false oppositions.

But the opposite of purity, as anthropologist Mary Douglas showed, is not just pollution—it is danger. All cultures set limits on sexuality because its power inspires fear—not just fear of pregnancy and disease, but of pollution, transgression, loss of control. Cutting off the end of the penis is only one way Judaism regulates this treacherous domain. Female sexuality must be regulated too, and unlike in some cultures—many millions of women in Africa have had their clitorises cut out and often their labia cut and partly sewed together—circumcision has no Jewish counterpart for female genitalia. But women regularly bleed from their wombs, and while the blood of virginity ended may seem amusing to some men, menstrual blood does not. Judaism—this time *like* many other cultures—deems this blood polluting and threatening.

It would be difficult to overstate the cultural importance of this judgment. Women are considered unclean for some twelve days each month if they are cycling normally. They may not be touched by any man, including their husbands, when they are in this state, and they must be purified by immersing themselves in a ritual bath, or *mikvah*, before this unclean period formally ends. Since this means no religious Jewish man may touch any woman whose menstrual status he doesn't know, almost any woman could be polluting. But in addition to the obvious limits on sexuality, the scope for limiting women's movements and interactions in order to prevent such pollution is very wide. Menstrual blood is the mortar with which the house of gender difference and gender bias is built.

This is also true in many other cultures throughout the world, and it can be viewed as just an excuse for excluding or oppressing women. But consider why menstruation might be frightening. It's not just that, as any teenage girl will tell you, it can be inconvenient and sometimes physically distressing—not to mention that men, who in many cultures can have no direct experience of it, seem to think it's yucky—or that it's blood, that red flag of injury and death. It's that for most of the past, regular menstruation after marriage was a very bad sign, regardless of culture. We think of it as a normal baseline state, and so it is today, but for most of our past, menstruation was much less common. Pregnant women don't do it, and breast-feeding women in the past suppressed it for a year or more after each birth. So women who birthed and breast-fed lots of babies had only a fraction—roughly a third—of the lifetime number of menstrual cycles most modern women do. In traditional cultures, persistent menstrual cycling begins to raise questions about fertility, and there are few worse things than childlessness for a woman in any traditional culture. So it's not for nothing that women call it "the curse."

For Jews, in a sense, menstrual blood matches the foreskin as a sign, symbol, and portent of infertility. As if pollution and infertility were not enough, Rabbinic tradition sees menses as part of Eve's punishment for her dawn-of-history sin. Not only are she and her daughters condemned to bring forth children in pain and suffering forever, but, *like murder-*

ers, women must be in a constant state of repentance for Eve's malfeasance, and menstruation serves as a regular reminder.[1]

Thus immersion in the *mikvah* is not a bath in the usual sense; in fact, every exposed cell of the body must be meticulously cleaned *before* the ritual, lest even the smallest spot be prevented by a speck of dirt from being touched by the purifying water. One nonreligious writer who spent a year with an Orthodox Jewish community described the experience this way:

> I take off the robe and stand expectantly in the chest-deep green water. Bracha tells me to keep my eyes and lips closed but not too tightly and to keep my feet and arms apart, so that the water will touch my whole body. When I go underwater I instantly curl into the fetal position. . . . I think of all the generations of people I have not known who have considered the impurities of the world dissolvable. My grandmother floats by, curled up, like me.[2]

Wasted semen is about as polluting as menstrual blood, so nocturnal emissions require a man to go to the *mikvah*, too. But these occur mainly in youth, so the stricture is less a part of a man's life cycle than a woman's. Still, there is a parallel here: As Onan spilled his seed on the ground instead of making a baby, so a menstruating woman spills her seed every month. And the prohibition of contact affects the sex lives of men and women alike. But paradoxically, observant men and women say that the twelve days of abstinence, how-

Entrance to an ancient *mikvah*, one of ten in Ramat
Rahel, Israel, dating to the Second Temple period.
Photograph by Todd Bolen, BiblePlaces.com. Used by permission.

ever frustrating, give them a keener appetite for sex and a
sweeter coupling. Romantically, they claim, the reunion is
like a monthly honeymoon. Certainly, a rhythm like this
might be counted on to generate a few sly looks and shy
smiles on days ten, eleven, and twelve, and the waiting
might be ripe with delicious temptations.

But the stricture against touching could be rigid and even
discourage tenderness. To get a feeling for how serious this
is, consider the experience of Glückel of Hameln, a great
Yiddish-language memoirist and leading businesswoman of
the early 1700s, when her deeply loved husband was on his
deathbed. A doctor came around midnight, but nothing fur-

ther could be done for him. "I said to my husband, 'Dearest heart, shall I embrace you—I am unclean?' For I was then at a time when I dared not touch him. And he said, 'God forbid, my child—it will not be long before you take your cleansing.' But alas, it was then too late."[3] They had been married thirty years and kept the law until the end.

Speaking of endings, even the purest bodies die and, untampered with, turn putrid very quickly, so what must be done with a lifeless body is strictly specified in Jewish law. According to the Torah, the corpse should be buried the same day, a commandment the Rabbis trace to the "dust to dust" condemnation of physically perfect Adam and Eve by God upon their expulsion from Paradise. When the soul is gone, the body is worse than nothing—dust—and must be gotten rid of immediately.

It's an interesting end for a body that, under Jewish law, has been treated as sacred from birth. If it's just dust, it must be a special sort of dust. Religious boys and men, at least, say a blessing on arising, thanking God for their having lived through the night, a blessing on washing, a blessing on completing urination or defecation, thanking God for the ongoing functioning of the physiological waterways, and as we have seen they are soon intoning a litany of further blessings thanking God for many other things as well. Women must observe the laws of menstrual cleanliness and, of course, must use their bodies for the most sacred purpose of all: making the next generation of Jewish children.

So the body from which life has departed, dust though it is, must be respected. It is ritually washed—many synagogues have groups of men and women (for male and female bodies respectively) who fulfill this law. They are called the *chevrah kadisha*, or sacred fellowship, and their task is *taharah*, or purification. These ministrations are called "acts of loving-kindness," and should not be left to professional undertakers. The deceased is dressed only in a white shroud, made simply of muslin or linen; this curtails any postmortem "keeping up with the Schwartzes" and declares that we are equal before God. Likewise, the shroud has no pockets because, well, you can't take it with you.

The body must never be left unattended. A *shomer*, or watcher, should sit up with it all night and read Psalms, traditionally to ward off evil spirits. A body must not be mutilated; autopsy is forbidden unless absolutely necessary and no preparations other than cleansing and purification are applied. (Organ donation is permitted because the highest value is placed on preserving a life, but that outcome has to be highly likely, the recipient must be a designated person who needs the organ, not an organ bank, and most important, the donor must be pronounced dead by standard criteria before the organ is removed.) Tattoos are forbidden even during life; Leviticus 19:28 states clearly, "You shall not make gashes in your flesh for the dead nor incise any marks on yourselves: I am the Lord." This strict prohibition of mutilation makes circumcision all the more striking.[4]

No more than a day or two must pass before the body is interred, in the same shroud, and at most in a plain pine box—the simpler the better. At the funeral the casket is closed. In absolute contrast to the ancient Egyptians who enslaved them, Jews make no effort at all to preserve the body after death; "unto dust shalt thou return" requires all speed. The Egyptians' beliefs about life after death led them to perfect the art and science of embalming and to bury their noble lords and ladies with objects of great value they would need for their future life. For the pharaohs, this might include slaves and servants murdered for the purpose of accompanying their master or mistress on the journey.

Jews consider embalming desecration; even before they distinguished their living bodies from those of the Greeks, they distinguished their dead ones from those of the Egyptians. For Jews, the body could not be preserved and was not worth preserving. In due course, upon the coming of the Messiah, the body might be revived, but in the meantime it should become dust again in the most natural way. It is considered ideal to be buried in only the shroud, and in various times and places—among the sixteenth-century Kabbalists, for example, and among Orthodox Jews in modern Israel— this ideal has been held to. Still, simple caskets have long been accepted. They should be of wood, not metal, because metal is used to make weapons and would not be consistent with resting in peace, and because it prevents the body's timely return to the earth. It was customary for the coffin to be of pine—soft, not hard, wood—and even to have holes drilled in the bottom, piercing the barrier between dust and dust.

The speed of burial is based on this and on two passages

in Deuteronomy 21:23: "You shall surely bury him the same day" and "His body shall not remain all night." The same-day requirement is officially stretched to twenty-four hours from the death—one night of watching—although compelling family or legal issues may permit a delay of at most three days. But a dead body, however properly prepared, is inherently impure; a descendant of priests, like his Temple ancestors, may not even go to a funeral. As long as a corpse is out of the ground, it blurs the ultimate boundary, the one between life and death.

At the conclusion of the graveside service the mourners themselves are expected to empty a shovelful of earth into the grave, a vestige of the custom—maintained among some traditional Jews today—of family members performing the entire burial. This implicates those who grieve as being resigned to the death and is a final, loving act, not to be delegated to a stranger. The shovel is not passed from hand to hand but stuck back into the ground as each mourner follows the last, to show that the shovel belongs to no one and that human beings have no control over death. Having helped to bury my mother, my father, and my wife, I can attest that it did seem loving, yet the sound of those clods thumping against the hollow box makes for a chilling drumbeat of finality. In other words, it served both purposes that it was intended to serve.

Throughout, it is considered proper to grieve openly over the loss; there is no stiff upper lip and no talk of the deceased's being in a better place, being resurrected, or being elevated to heaven—despite the Jewish belief that for a righteous person (Jewish or not) life after death is somehow better than life on earth. The famous Kaddish prayer makes not the least allusion to death or the deceased but simply praises God, lest grief make the mourner forget to fulfill this obligation in letter and spirit, or worse, blame or curse God. The mourners' loss should be palpable, but not their anger. The law requires that a garment be cut and then torn in a place close to or opposite the heart; many Jews commonly substitute a tear in a black ribbon pinned to the garment. This may sublimate any impulse to cut or tear at one's own flesh out of grief—accepted in some cultures, but for Jews a sacrilege against the living body.

After the burial, the hands are washed ceremonially. Mourners sit quietly on low stools at home for seven days, receive visitors, and hold three prayer services a day. This "sitting shivah" (shivah being related to both the word for seven and the word for rest) entails specific demands on the bodies of the living. Mourners should eat immediately after returning from the cemetery, with food provided by others—the "Meal of Condolence"—lest they fail to sustain their own bodies out of grief. They are not allowed to shave, have sex, bathe more than minimally, wash their clothes, or wear leather shoes, and mirrors in the house of mourning are covered over, a custom variously explained as a rejection of vanity, a protection from seeing oneself in such a terrible state, and a superstition about the tendency of the soul of the mourner to leave the body through the mirror during a time when the life-death boundary is blurred. Meanwhile, at the cemetery, the return to dust should already have begun.

6

God's Beard

Not least because bodies die and putrify, a bodiless God was an article of Jewish faith, and this may shed light on how the Jews viewed their own all-too-human bodies. The flesh of the Greek gods may have been incorruptible, but the Jewish God had no flesh to corrupt. We are always at risk for becoming dirty in our bodies, while God is serenely pure because he doesn't have one. Yet there seems to be room in the Torah, and in subsequent Jewish tradition, for doubt.

We are created in God's image, the Bible says. Adam and Eve can hear God's voice as He walks in the garden. Does this mean God has legs? Noah, after the flood, "built an altar to the Lord and . . . offered burnt offerings on the altar. The Lord smelled the pleasing odor, and the Lord said to Himself: 'Never again will I doom the earth because of man.' "[1] (Gen. 8:20–21). God here seems almost to revert to pagan status, able to be swayed by bribes pleasing to His senses. And Moses, after begging for the privilege, is allowed briefly to see God's back. Carefully instructing him how he can do this without dying, God refers to His own face and hand:

"But," He said, "you cannot see My face, for man may not see Me and live." And the Lord said, "See, there is a place near Me. Station yourself on the rock and, as My Presence passes by, I will put you in a cleft of the rock and shield you with My hand until I have passed by. Then I will take My hand away and you will see My back; but My face must not be seen." (Exod. 33:20–23)

This is no commentary but the Torah text itself. And there is an even stranger reference, shortly after God has given the Israelites the Torah in the wilderness of Sinai. Moses dashes the people with the blood of sacrificed bulls, calling it "the blood of the covenant," and then, "Moses and Aaron . . . and seventy elders of Israel ascended; and they saw the God of Israel: under His feet there was the likeness of a pavement of sapphire. . . . Yet He did not raise His hand against the leaders of the Israelites; they beheld God, and they ate and drank" (Exod. 24:9–11).

Later Bible passages seem to confirm that God has a bodily form, although only very special people can see it. The prophet Micaiah says, "I saw the Lord seated upon His throne" (1 Kings 22:19); Isaiah says, "I beheld my Lord seated on a high and lofty throne; and the skirts of His robe filled the Temple" (Isa. 6:1); and Ezekiel describes a heavenly host whose wings sound like mighty waters or the din of an army. But he goes on:

Above the expanse over their heads was the semblance of a throne, in appearance like sapphire; and on top,

upon this semblance of a throne, there was the semblance of a human form. From what appeared as His
loins up, I saw a gleam as of amber—what looked like a
fire encased in a frame; and from what appeared as His
loins down, I saw what looked like fire. There was a
radiance all about Him. Like the appearance of the bow
which shines in the clouds on a day of rain, such was
the appearance of the surrounding radiance. That was
the appearance of the semblance of the Presence of the
Lord. When I beheld it, I flung myself down on my face.
And I heard the voice of someone speaking. (Ezek.
1:26–28)

The voice, too, was God's. Amos says, "I saw my Lord standing by the altar" (Amos 9:1). And Daniel says, "As I looked
on, Thrones were set in place, / And the Ancient of Days
took His seat. / His garment was like white snow, / The hair
of His head was like lamb's wool" (Dan. 7:9).

All in all, we have descriptions or allusions to God's
voice, nostrils, face, hand, back, loins, and feet, certainly "a semblance of human form" that speaks, walks,
smells, passes by, covers someone with his hand, wears
clothes, and sits on a throne. Most important, God brought
the people out of Egypt "with an outstretched arm" (Exod.
6:6). It is as if the Hebrews (and later the Jews), having formally rejected all embodied gods, felt a lingering need to

give human shape to their one Deity, in whose image they were made; and perhaps in doing so they brought God closer and made Him more comprehensible.

Most later Jewish theologians rejected these intimations of God's body—not the text itself of course, but the notion that they were anything but metaphors. But some in the Jewish mystical tradition took a more complex view. As far back as Talmud times, a text called *Shi'ur Komah*, or "the measurement of the Divine dimension,"[2] specifies the actual size of God's limbs and body, and they are huge. For example, it says that the entire universe hangs from God's arm like an amulet, an interpretation of the Torah passage, "and beneath his arm, the universe."[3] The book promises great rewards for those who study and master it; among other, more spiritual dividends: "He who recites this secret shall have a glowing face and an attractive body and his fear shall be cast upon his fellow men and his good name shall go among all Israel."[4]

The rabbis of the Kabbalah were more circumspect but equally willing to describe God, for their own reasons. Metaphorically, at least, they gave God a body, diagramming God's ten attributes in the shape of a human form. Remarkably, this form was part male and part female, just as the attributes were. After millennia of abstractions, the Kabbalists created a sort of abstract concreteness, mystical, strange, and beautiful, to satisfy just a little the human wish for a visible God. Even to the Kabbalists, God was unfathomable, "a face within a face, an essence within an essence, and a form within a form."[5] Rabbi Joseph Gikatilla, a medieval Spanish Kabbalist, wrote:

What are the words we read in the Torah . . . such as "hand," "leg," "ear," "eye" etc.? Realise and believe that even though these terms testify to His truth and His greatness, no creature can begin to understand the meaning of those entities called "hand," "leg," or "ear." Just because we were created in His own image and likeness, don't think that the eye which is written in the Torah is really a human eye, or that the hand is truly a human hand.[6]

Still, they devoted centuries to trying to grasp God's essence and to give it a mystical form. God, they believed, had attributes—*sefirot*—which they named and accorded distinct identities.

Finally, the Kabbalists drew not just bodies but several metaphoric structures relating God's attributes to one another and (of course) to the unitary whole. One of these was a geometric diagram with an octagon at the center, another a cosmic tree, yet another, a river giving rise to many streams. But the strangest and the most challenging to traditional Jewish ideas of God is the one in which the *sefirot* are parts of God's very human-looking body. Yes, God at the outset made human beings "in our image"—a puzzling phrase in itself—but for centuries the typical Rabbinic interpretation of this was spiritual or intellectual.

Still, there are those pesky biblical references to God's face, hands, back, feet, even loins, and some Rabbis always thought that "in our image" was somehow about the body, too. The Kabbalists, with their mystical bent, drew the logical conclusion of trying to imagine God's body as an assemblage of God's attributes. The first was the *Ein Sof*—the "No End," from which all the others emanate. Divine Will, Wisdom, Intelligence, Love, Judgment, Endurance, Majesty, and Righteousness are of roughly equal importance, but a ninth, called Beauty or Compassion, is given a privileged place, as is Divine Presence—Shekhinah—the feminine aspect, which gives God an almost maternal side.

In one humanlike depiction, a figure called *Adam Kadmon*—primordial man—stands in for God. This is the superhuman Adam who, according to tradition, was originally created to be a projection of God and the repository of all human souls, as large in size as Noah's Ark. As conceptualized and depicted in Kabbalah, *Adam Kadmon* clearly contains the same sacred attributes that the mystic Rabbis accorded to God.

Three of the attributes make up the head, three the arms and chest, and three the legs and genitals, while the tenth represents the whole harmony. Another bodily drawing shows the figure divided vertically, the left side representing God's feminine essence and the right side the masculine. Oddly, love in this model is on the masculine side and judgment on the feminine. If these were in part the projections of the mystics' own bodies onto what they imagined to be God's, then they inevitably had much to say about our human essence as well. As the great modern Kabbalah scholar Gershom Scholem put it, "both man and God encompass within their being the entire cosmos. . . . What exists seminally in God unfolds and develops in man. . . .

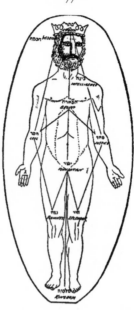

Adam Kadmon, the superhuman first man, depicted as
embodying the attributes of God, according to the
Rabbis of Kabballah, the great works of Jewish
mysticism.

Man is the perfecting agent in the structure of the cosmos;
like all the other created beings, only even more so, he is
composed of all ten *Sefirot* and 'of all spiritual things.' "[7]

The female aspect of God, Shekhinah, or "Divine Presence," is one of God's most important attributes. Rabbi
Joseph wrote of Shekhinah, "She so pervades this lower
world that if you search in deed, speech, thought, and specu-
lation, you will find *Shekhinah*, for there is no beginning nor
end to her."[8] Her cheeks are like bright red apples and her
hair is black, curly, and oiled. "In each tress hang many

strands, and each strand illumines many worlds." She is Israel's comfort in exile; indeed, she herself is exiled with the Jewish people, and their suffering is hers. But she can be very dangerous, because despite her main nature—gentle, maternal, and understanding—she can be separated from the rest of God, whereupon she becomes a particularly fierce kind of Judgment, now red with anger, her many-stranded hair filled with the power to destroy. In Rabbi Joseph's conception, the letters of the Torah itself are the links, some symbolically but explicitly sexual, which unite the King and Queen of the universe. One main purpose of sexual intercourse, according to the sixteenth-century Kabbalist Isaac Luria, is to keep them together.[9] Torah study strengthens the links and woe to humanity if they break apart.

Given these images, it is perhaps not surprising that the scholar's relationship to the Torah came to be seen as a love affair: The Torah

> may be compared to a beautiful and stately maiden, who is secluded in an isolated chamber of a palace, and has a lover. . . . For love of her he passes by her gate unceasingly, and turns his eyes in all directions to discover her. She is aware that he is forever hovering about the palace. . . . She thrusts open a small door in her secret chamber, for a moment reveals her face to her lover, then quickly withdraws it . . . but he is aware it is from love of him that she has revealed herself to him for that moment, and his heart and his soul and everything within him are drawn to her.

The metaphor is explained and extended:

> So it is with the Torah. . . . She knows that whosoever
> is wise in heart hovers near the gates of her dwelling
> place day after day. . . . From her palace, she shows her
> face to him, and gives him a signal of love . . . if he
> fails, [she] says to her messengers: Go tell that simple-
> ton to come to me, and converse . . . she commences to
> speak with him, at first from behind the veil which she
> has hung before her words. . . . Then she speaks to him
> behind a filmy veil of finer mesh, she speaks to him in
> riddles and allegories. . . .
>
> When, finally he is on near terms with her, she
> stands disclosed face to face with him, and holds con-
> verse with him concerning all of her secret mysteries,
> and all the secret ways which have been hidden in her
> heart from immemorial time.[10]

Such was the sacredness and purity of these men's love for
God and Torah that they could use romantic and sexual
metaphors to demonstrate their passion and their tenderness without becoming uneasy; such was their respect for
sex and love that these comparisons did not in the least sully
their relationship with God. On the contrary, since God
placed a similarly high value on marital union, these
metaphors could only seem a gesture of respect.

Like the hair of the Shekhinah, the beard of God was said
to be black, curled, oily, and full of mysteries. As the mystic
scholar became mighty in the art of contemplation, he
became lost in the thirteen curls of the cosmic beard. He

could climb to higher and higher levels within it, and in one of the most marvelous metaphors in Judaism, we are asked to think of the most spiritually adept rabbis as flowing along in the sacred, brightly lit, oiled channels of God's vast, intricate, dark, beautiful, and finally unfathomable beard.

7

"Hath Not a Jew Eyes?"

It is interesting that a people ridiculed for their looks for many centuries should from Bible times have placed a high value on physical beauty; and in contrast to both circumcision (a required completion) and tattooing (a forbidden desecration), most efforts to enhance physical beauty were simply permitted. Of course, beauty is relative, and always is in part in the eye of the beholder. When the beholders were more numerous and more powerful, they defined downward the Jews' physical appearance even more than some Jews defined non-Jewish appearance up, and both definitions had serious consequences. To the Greeks and Romans, with their Apollonian ideal, Jews were deformed and hopeless as competitors, and their cultural heirs have dominated Europe ever since.

Among the countless beholders who belittled and despised the Jews are unfortunately quite a few great and near-great men and women in the English language literary tradition.[1] Dickens presents Fagin in *Oliver Twist* as "a very old shrivelled Jew, whose villainous looking and repulsive face was obscured by a quantity of red matted hair." In

Nostromo, Joseph Conrad offers up a Jew named Hirsch who, we are often reminded, has "a hooked beak," an almost pathological cowardice, and a "practical mercantile soul." George Bernard Shaw's representative Jew in *Man and Superman* is Mendoza, a bandit chief with "striking cockatoo nose, glossy black hair . . . and Mephisthophelean [i.e. devilish] affectation." D. H. Lawrence, in *The Virgin and the Gipsy*, describes "a very small woman with a rather large nose: probably a Jewess . . . her wide, rather resentful brown eyes of a spoilt Jewess gazed oddly out of her expensive get-up . . . eyes that had still the canny shrewdness of a bourgeois Jewess: a rich one probably . . . she was in love, in a Jewess's curious way."

The list goes on. And on. The stereotype is clear: "The Jew" has beady (small), closely set eyes; a large hooked nose; big protruding ears; a set of wet, bulbous, protruding lips; dark curly hair; oily or "greasy" hair and skin; short stature; a round, bulging belly; and a dark ("swarthy") complexion—except of course when the Jew's skin is deemed pathologically pale due to lack of healthy outdoor activities. Less anatomically descriptive adjectives such as insidious, repulsive, pathological, underhanded, devious, sinister, evasive, odious, accursed, loathsome, sneaky, ill-shapen, restless, obnoxious, self-willed, obstinate, flashy, gaudy, boisterous, egotistical, pushy, overbearing, aggressive, lustful, rapacious, greedy, perfidious, unscrupulous, spineless, obsequious, obtrusive, repugnant, suspicious, villainous, abominable, shriveled, devilish, Mephisthophelean, and so on are interwoven with descriptions of visible body organs to blur the line between objective and subjective description and to lend the substantial negative emotive power of words and phrases describing character to what might otherwise be more neutral descriptions of shape, size, texture, and color.

One of the strangest of all ideas about the Jewish body began in the Middle Ages and came down at least to the streets of Brooklyn where I was growing up in the 1950s: Non-Jewish boys would sometimes taunt us with the demand that we show them our horns, and they seemed to believe that the purpose of our yarmulkes and other head coverings was to conceal the stubs of the cut-off horns. Since the Devil and some of his imps have horns, this belief confirmed their worst fears about the "Satanic" Jews and their insidious aims of corrupting good Christians and dominating the world.

Just as we owe the epithet "Shylock" to the greatest playwright of all time, we owe our horns largely to the greatest Renaissance artist. Michelangelo's statue of Moses, coming down from Mount Sinai with the tablets of the Law cradled in his arm, has quite prominent horns. Surely Michelangelo did not mean to associate the Ten Commandments with deviltry, nor to challenge the prevailing Christian reverence for Moses and his Law?

It turns out that it was all a big mistake, due to a mistranslation of the Torah text by Saint Jerome, whose Latin-language version of the Jewish Bible was the first directly translated from the Hebrew. Exodus, chapter 34, says repeatedly that "*karan or panav,*" which the translators of the King James Version correctly rendered "the skin of his face shone." The rays coming from his face were so intense that Moses had to don a veil to protect the people's eyes. Unfortunately, the word *karan* can mean either "ray" or "horn," depending on the context, and Saint Jerome rather fancifully gave Moses the horns that Michelangelo faithfully carved in stone, and that became a staple of anti-Semitic depictions of Jews ever since.

Of course, the Jews of Europe did on average look different from the people around them, but any physical descriptions themselves apply to only a subset of Jews, and the variation is enormous. In fact, there is great overlap between the physical characteristics of Jews and those of others, not least because of the more than occasional Jewish import-export trade in genes. However, as we have seen, most of us don't think in terms of probabilities or statistical distributions, but in categories and types. So when those who write for average readers or playgoers perpetuate stereotypes, they are practicing and encouraging a more primitive kind of thought—a kind of thought that, applied to human variation and human groups, has had massive tragic consequences.

Even Shakespeare, in his—there is no escaping it—fundamentally anti-Semitic play *The Merchant of Venice*, gives the moneylender Shylock many stereotypic character traits. Yet he also lets him defend himself and his tribe against their enemies' definition of the Jewish body:

I am a Jew. Hath not a Jew eyes? Hath not a Jew hands, organs, dimensions, senses, affections, passions; fed with the same food, hurt with the same weapons, subject to the same diseases, heal'd by the same means, warm'd and cool'd by the same winter and summer as a Christian is? If you prick us, do we not bleed? If you tickle us, do we not laugh? If you poison us, do we not die? And if you wrong us, shall we not revenge? (3.1.58).

How very physical this is. The opening sentence suggests that what follows will define "a Jew," and Shylock's defensive definition deems him no different, biologically, than any other member of the sorry human race. And the last, dramatically crucial sentence implies that even the very behavior that makes him so hateful and hated in the play is a normal, predictable part of biological human nature.

Indeed, the whole play is anatomical, turning as it does on the Jew's contemptible demand for his literal pound of flesh. Sneering insistently and stupidly almost until the end, the insidiously clever Jew is outgamed by one of Shakespeare's most fully developed, dazzlingly brilliant (not to mention desirable) women. Sure, she says, take your pound of flesh, but if you take one drop of blood, or one iota more or less than a pound, your life is done.

No longer allowed to withdraw, he forfeits all his wealth to save his life. But the most painful punishment, and the one with the greatest human and biblical significance, is Shylock's loss of his own flesh and blood—his only child, the surpassingly lovely, Gentile-tempting (and Gentile-tempted) Jessica. She converts, rejecting her and her father's ancient covenant, cutting Shylock off from the future of his people just as surely as if he had not been circumcised, as if he himself had broken the covenant.

Pouring salt on his open wound, the duke (on the selfless advice of Antonio, Shylock's debtor and intended victim) rules that the half of his wealth that does not go to the state will go to his daughter's Christian husband—"the gentleman that lately stole his daughter"—ensuring that Shylock himself will fund the Christianization of his descendants. Reneging on his pardon, the duke holds that Shylock will die if he doesn't convert; not exactly Christian, but persuasive. Like many Jews before and since, given this forced choice, Shylock, too, becomes a Christian, with the words, "I am content," but he soon pleads illness and goes away; these decrees have broken his Jewish body.

Not so the fair Jessica, who opens the last act with a delicious, dreamy love scene. Indeed, several scenes before his moving self-defense, she has already betrayed him; she states her position clearly:

> Alack, what heinous sin is it in me
> To be ashamed to be my father's child!
> But though I am a daughter to his blood
> I am not to his manners. O Lorenzo
> If thou keep promise, I shall end this strife
> Become a Christian and thy loving wife. (2.3.16).

At least she still considers violating the fifth commandment a sin. But a recent performance I saw compounded the loss by making Jessica cross herself and wear a cross as a pendant around her neck, showing no ambivalence at all about the conversion—interpretive choices that the play does not in the least require. As the father of two daughters, I found that her gesture went through me like a knife.

But blood is blood and will often out. Will Jessica be destined to be accepted as a Christian, or will her children and grandchildren bear the ongoing taint of the blood of the Jew? The historical record does not urge optimism, even for the honorable convert. Controversy continues over what the Spanish attitude was toward Jewish converts to Christianity at the time of and after the mass expulsion in 1492. But it seems likely that there was a racist element in the Inquisition, which, in the guise of outing and burning "Judaizers," was really identifying new Christians and their descendants with the taint not just of Jewish belief but of Jewish blood.[2] In such a case, even though the Jewish soul may have been purged, the Jewish body still had to be destroyed.

Whether or not this was true of the Inquisition, it became the essence of European anti-Semitism by the late nineteenth century. That century, beginning with the Enlightenment and especially with Napoleon's historic and forceful emancipation of the Jews, appeared to be an era of growing freedom and equality for this traditionally isolated and downtrodden people. But by the 1880s, a virulent anti-Semitism was metastasizing in Europe. In the backward East it took the most obvious form: murderous pogroms such as had not been seen since the 1600s.

In the first few years of the new century, many thousands of defenseless Jewish men, women, and children were murdered in hundreds of communities where their non-Jewish neighbors rioted against them. In a single week in 1905 there were more than fifty pogroms in Czarist Russia. The pattern

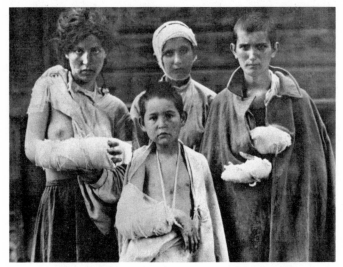

Survivors of the 1919 riot against the Jews of Khodorkov,
Ukraine, photographed at the hospital in Kiev. It was
one of more than 1,300 such pogroms against Jews during
the Russian revolution, which caused 70,000 deaths and
led to the Third Aliya, or wave of immigration to Israel.
Jewish National University Library, Jerusalem. Used by permission.

was repeated around fifteen years later during and after the
Russian civil war. Contemplating the wreckage of their lives
and the threats around them, many Russian, Ukrainian, and
other East European Jews began to move away, some to
American dreams, and some to a much more challenging life
in what was then called Palestine. In fact, each of these three
waves of murderous riots stimulated a major wave of immigration to the embryonic but growing Jewish nation. All this
seemed an immense tragedy at the time but was nothing
compared with the organized mass murders to come.

8

Race and Destiny

Of course, the effective practice of anti-Semitism is demanding; among other things, it requires that you learn how to identify a Jew, and this is not always easy. One dimension of the Passover story is that Moses was able to pass not just for Egyptian but for Egyptian nobility. There must have been, in his body, face, and bearing, little or no evidence of his lowly Hebrew origins. He was accepted as an Egyptian prince until he himself decided that his life and fate belonged to his own people.

Yet in the past few centuries, despite the effort that has gone into physically defining a Jewish race, some of the bitterest vitriol has been reserved for Jews who *don't* look like "Jews." These impostors, goes the rhetoric, are even more insidious than typical, obvious Jews, since they are infecting, infesting the collective body of "normal" people without being found out, a kind of latent virus that can linger for years or decades in a healthy-seeming communal body and then spring forth in vicious attacks.

This was, perhaps, the twentieth century's most destructive metaphor. Building on the racial tracts of the nine-

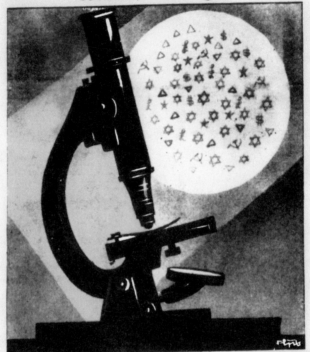

"Infectious Germs." From the Nazi propaganda organ *Der Stürmer*, April 15, 1943. The poem: "With his poison, the Jew drags / Weaker peoples' burdened blood, / So a disease-picture appears / That speeds them downward. / But our report resounds: / The blood is clean. We're healthy!"

teenth century, German physicians and scientists gradually turned the Jews into a health problem by defining Jews themselves as a disease. For instance, a drawing in *Der Stürmer*, a principal Nazi propaganda tabloid, in April 1942, showed a large microscope in profile, under the title "Infectious Germs"; above the instrument a round white microscope field; and drawn on the field—many small hammer-and-sickle symbols, triangles (for homosexuals), and, most prominently, Stars of David.

Even many who know quite a lot about the Holocaust don't realize that it was in essence a public health project. Jews were diseased, of course, but more important, they *were* a disease. "Modern science" taught that genes are the foundation of all health, and Jewish genes were destroying the health of the German race. Intermarriage between Jews and other Germans had increased. "Pure" German birthrates had declined. Jews were contaminating other Germans with many viral and bacterial diseases, but worst of all they were contaminating the German race with their genes. These things were measurable, measured, and aggressively brought to the attention of the German people.

In essence, this was a public health crisis, and German physicians and scientists rose to the occasion.[1] Doctors were among the first, most enthusiastic, and most loyal of Nazis—after, that is, they had purged their ranks of Jewish colleagues. German medical scientists were *the* most important intellectual pillars of the Nazi war against the Jews. Dr. Josef Mengele, M.D., Ph.D., was not stationed at Auschwitz just to decide who should be murdered by gassing immediately and who looked healthy enough to be worth working to death. He was there as a medical, public health, and racial expert, to certify that every Jew sent to the gas chambers was murdered for health reasons—the health of the pure German race. Nazi mass murder needed a doctor's signature on what was, in effect, a prescription for German health. So central was this theory that Hitler, in a 1935 propaganda picture, was depicted bending down tenderly in a field of flowers face-to-face with a charming little girl—she could have been Heidi herself—with the legend: "*Adolf Hitler als Artzt des deutsche Volkes*"—"Adolf Hitler, doctor of the German people."

Real public health measures were constantly conflated with racist theory. Health care was to be replaced by health leadership, curative measures by preventive ones, and personal by racial hygiene. This was not some small fringe group of German doctors and scientists but the overwhelming majority. The countless courses they taught on genetics and public health at the best universities, the richly supported journals, laboratories, and institutes, the thousands of "studies" they conducted to "test" these vacuous theories made the Nazi view of the Jewish body the intellectual norm throughout Germany, and later throughout the vast Nazi empire. The Reich Health Publishing House boasted that in 1939 alone it used some 924 metric tons of paper (ninety-two boxcar loads), enough to stretch three-fourths of the way around the earth. "Scientific" books and articles presented "evidence" that Jews were more afflicted by many diseases than non-Jews were, and that their inferior genes were responsible.

Hitler himself had laid the foundation in his early memoir *Mein Kampf* (*My Struggle*). From his youth he was obsessed with the Jewish racial threat:

> With satanic joy in his face, the black-haired Jewish youth lurks in wait for the unsuspecting girl whom he defiles with his blood, thus stealing her from her people. With every means he tries to destroy the racial foundations of the people he has set out to subjugate. Just as he himself systematically ruins women and girls, he does not shrink back from pulling down the blood barriers for others, even on a large scale. It was and it is Jews who bring the Negroes into the Rhineland, always with the same secret thought and clear aim of ruining the hated white race by the necessarily resulting bastardization, throwing it down from its cultural and political height, and himself rising to be its master.

Thus in the early 1920s, Adolf Hitler thought that the Jewish threat was partly that Jews, "with satanic joy," "ruin" Aryan women with their contaminated blood, and partly that they lowered the barriers for people of African descent, "with the . . . clear aim of ruining the hated white race."

This view had been rendered scientifically plausible by Houston Stewart Chamberlain, whose treatises *Foundations of the Nineteenth Century*—first published in German translation as *Grundlagen des neunzehnten Jahrhunderts*—and *Race and Nation* argued that the fall and rise of nations could best be understood by reference to the coming and going of Jews.

Cartoon from Dr. Kurt Plischke's *Der Jude als
Rassenschaender: Eine Anklage gegen Juda und eine Mahnung
an die deutschen Frauen und Maedchen* (The Jew as Race
Defiler: An Accusation against Judah and a Warning to
German Women and Girls). Germany, circa 1935.
*Courtesy of the United States Holocaust Memorial Museum,
used by permission of the USHMM Photo Archives.*

The impact was racial; the Jews contaminated European
nations with their bad blood.

These books were widely discussed among German students from the time they were first published.[2] Anti-Semitic
posters complete with swastikas, with the theme of Jews
polluting German women, appeared on the wall of the
Reichstag, the German parliament, as early as 1920. Alfred

Rosenberg, Hitler's adviser during the Nazi movement's early years, called Chamberlain's work "the strongest positive impulse in my youth," and prepared excerpts of *Foundations of the Nineteenth Century* for Hitler's easy study.[3] Heinrich Himmler, later and throughout the war the head of the SS and a key figure in all concentration and killing operations, read *Race and Nation* at the end of 1921 and recorded his thoughts about it in his diary: "It is true and one has the impression that it is objective, not just hate-filled anti-Semitism. Because of this it has more effect. These terrible Jews."[4] With this in mind, the Nazis had a noble task ahead of them and a heavy responsibility: prevent "these terrible Jews" from further contaminating the superior races of Europe and thus protect the future of the world.

In the end it was all about the body. Most instructive is a charmingly illustrated children's book called *Der Giftpilz* (*The Poison Mushroom*), first published in 1938.[5] It went through several editions and hundreds of thousands of copies. The vivid cover drawing shows Jews as toadstools, with ugly Jewish faces instead of stems. The second story, "How Do We Know the Jew?" is about a particularly lively lesson in a seventh-grade class. The translation is by Randall Bytwerk.

> The teacher is telling about the Jews. . . . Little Karl takes hold of a pointer, goes up to the blackboard, and points to the drawings.
>
> "We usually know the Jew by his nose. The Jewish nose is crooked at its point. It looks like a six. That's why it's called the Jewish six. Many non-Jews also have bent

Der Giftpilz (The Poison Mushroom), a children's book
published in Germany in 1938 by *Der Stürmer Verlag*,
Julius Streicher's anti-Semitic publishing house.
Used by permission of Dr. Randall Bytwerk, The German Propaganda Archive,
www.calvin.edu/academic/cas/gpa.

noses. But with them the nose is not bent underneath,
but farther up. We call that kind of nose a hook-nose or
eagle-nose. It has nothing to do with the Jewish nose."

"Quite right!" says the teacher. "But it's not just by
his nose that we know the Jew . . ."

The boy explains further. "We also know the Jew by
his lips. His lips are usually puffy. Often the lower lip
hangs out a bit. That's called 'sloppy.' And by the eyes
too we can recognize Jews. His eyelids are usually

thicker and fleshier than ours. The glance of the Jew is sneaky and penetrating. We can see right away that he is a false person."

The knowledge is precise and anatomical. The teacher now calls on Fritz, the best student in the class, who picks up where Karl left off, pointing out that Jews tend to be small to medium height, bow-legged and flat-footed with short legs and arms. They often have a low, slanting forehead, a receding forehead like many criminals—which the Jews are, too. Big ears like cup handles and dark, curly hair are other identifying features. Praising Fritz, the teacher asks the others why the boy had used qualifying adjectives such as "tend to" and "often." A big, strong boy in the last row named Heinrich explains that they may have the big ears but not the nose, the eyes but not the feet. Some are even blond. You have to look closely, but if you do, you can always tell a Jew. Yet another boy, blond and smiling, lists the Jew's behavioral traits: a shuffling, unsteady gait, prattling on in a peculiar nasal voice while moving his head and hands, and smelling unpleasantly sweet; if you have a good nose, he says, you can smell them. Approving all this, the teacher leads the class in a group recitation of a poem in which the Jew is described as a wicked Devil, an evil plague in every country, from whom young people must fight to be free.

But the book's title story makes it clear that identifying Jews is not always easy. A mother gathers mushrooms in the forest with her son but must teach him very well; poison mushrooms and edible ones may look very much alike. In a tedious didactic homily she emphasizes the main point to bright and eager little Franz: the Jew is the most poisonous mushroom of all.

Der Giftpilz is just one item in a vast program of books, articles, posters, speeches, meetings, rallies, youth groups, classes, exhibits, plays, radio shows, and films that brought this lesson home to Germans of all ages and stations in life, and then to many millions of other Europeans. The catechism of poisonous evil Jews as the world's plague was elicited everywhere, and learning the facial and bodily signs of Jewish identity had practical and ideological value. Furthermore, every item in this anatomical list was the product of "scientific" research and analysis in institutions that were Germany's intellectual pinnacles.

One of the most important instruments of propaganda and social control was film, which by the 1930s had reached a level of technical sophistication that was difficult for many viewers to resist. In addition to heavily dramatized documentary films of Nazi rallies, there were films vividly depicting the evil of the Jews. *Jud Süss* was a Nazi transformation of an old novel.[6] In the novel the Jew, named Süss, does underhanded business dealings that cause a death, and though he learns in the end he is not Jewish, he elects to suffer persecution as if he were. But in the film he is satanically and viciously Jewish; audiences cheered his execution by hanging at the end.

A "documentary" called *The Eternal Jew* (*Der Ewige Jude*) was at least equally influential.[7] Jewish children have no idealism; Palestine is the international center of world Jewry;

Jews are the ultimate mixed race, combining Asian, European, and even "a hint of the Negroid"; Jews control 82 percent of crime and 98 percent of prostitution; they caused the inflation that plagued Germany; they produce degenerate art—"fevered fantasies of incurably sick minds" (as illustrated in the film by great works of cubism and abstract expressionism); they perverted German theater and glorified child murderers in their films; they perverted science (as illustrated by Albert Einstein); and they deliberately torture animals with their kosher butchering. All these themes are spoken in voice-over while many prurient and disgusting images are shown, including instructive illustrations of how Jews try to disguise themselves. Perhaps the centerpiece of the film is the sequence in which rats stand in for Jews, crowding on top of each other, spreading throughout the world, "found mostly in large packs," bringing "disease, plague, leprosy, typhoid fever, cholera, dysentery, and so on." The film ends with a montage of the German people—clean, handsome, noble, and glorious yet threatened relentlessly by the insidious Jewish menace.

One of the searing ironies of the Third Reich's success is that it eventually did turn many Jews into real threats to public health. Before they were sent to be murdered in gas chambers they were dragged, shoved, beaten, and crammed into impossibly crowded ghettos where typhus, typhoid fever, dysentery, tuberculosis, and other highly contagious diseases raged, leaving corpses in the streets. The Germans turned the Jewish body into a disease-infested threat to "Aryans" outside the ghettos. Auschwitz at its height could murder over twenty thousand people in a day, yet millions had to wait their turn in these plague-swept urban prisons, for weeks, months, even years, dying by German design.

ampshade farming" was my nickname for Jewish child-rearing for some months after my first child was born. To say that this joke was not to my wife's taste is putting it mildly, so I soon kept it to myself. Millions of Jews are thinking thoughts we do not express. You cannot live in a Jewish body after the Holocaust without being troubled by such musings about that body's nature and fate at the hands of others who can define it at will. Like people living on the San Andreas Fault, or in other places prone to earthquakes, volcanic eruptions, hurricanes, tornados, forest fires, mudslides, and the like, Jews aware of their history live with the ongoing sense that a social or societal quake may make non-Jews their enemies more or less overnight. And since those others are far more numerous, our vulnerability is obvious. The social structure may suddenly shift beneath us, leaving us scrambling rather desperately for a foothold. It is not a paranoid fantasy, it's a historical reality. It probably can't happen "here," we think, but then again perhaps it can.

The Nazis' plan of identification, isolation, persecution, torture, and murder of the Jews was obsessively embodied. They thought the Jews were ugly but made them much uglier, by imposing the yellow star, driving them into poverty-stricken ghettos, starving them, and inflicting infectious disease on them, killing them almost as surely as if they had injected them with typhus (which, in "experimental" settings, they later did). When the mass murders by shooting began, they made the Jews strip naked first, and, like most of us who are not young athletes, actors, dancers, or models, they looked worse naked than dressed. This made mass murder easier, as did the collective graves they fell into when they were shot.

A non-Jewish Polish journalist kept a diary of the process by which the Jews of Vilna, Lithuania, were murdered in a forest area near the city: "1942. July 30, Friday. About one hundred and fifty persons shot. Most of them were elderly people. The executioners complained about being very tired of their 'work,' of having aching shoulders from shooting. That is the reason for not finishing the wounded off, so that they are buried alive." Like most of their anti-Jewish operations, some Germans documented this process in film and photographs; they were doing the world a favor and took pride in it.

Gas chambers refined the techniques. Jews were now stripped and shorn of their hair, allegedly so they could be disinfected, and lined up for the "showers." According to an affidavit filed by Rudolf Höss, commandant of Auschwitz, "Babies who interfered with the shaving of their mother's hair were grabbed by the legs and smashed against the wall. Upon occasion the guard handed the bloody mess to the mother."[8] The Germans amassed (and photographed) huge piles of eyeglasses and wedding rings;

these, like the mountains of human hair, were sent to market. Apparently the hair of the women of this inferior race could be made into suitable wigs for German ladies. Certainly the gold could be pried from their lifeless mouths and melted down to underwrite the Master Race and its selfless, world-purifying ambitions.

Systematic deceptions were close to the heart of the enterprise and took interesting advantage of the physical self-image of the Jews, always low but now worsened by years of severe deprivation. *"Arbeit Macht Frei"*—"Work Makes You Free"—was famously emblazoned over the gateway to Auschwitz, an effort to reassure some Jews that the Nazis were just trying to strengthen them and make them more German. After centuries of stereotyping that depicted Jews as sickly weaklings who avoided both physical labor and fighting, *"Arbeit Macht Frei"* must have seemed an almost logical turn of phrase. As these ill, starving people stood naked in their final lines, they must have been impressed with the strength and bearing of the uniformed German soldiers. On the way into the gas chamber itself, an SS man told the Jews, "Breathe deeply, it strengthens the lungs."[9] They were holding receipts for their clothing.

Whips backed up the lies, and Jews were packed into the chamber like sardines. Gas pellets hit the floor. Naked victims clambered over each other to reach the remaining air, but in four minutes all were dead. "The bodies were found in tower-like heaps, some in sitting or half-sitting position. . . . The corpses were pink in color, with green spots. Some had foam on their lips; others bled through the nose."[10] Gold fill-

April 28, 1945. Some of the 60,000 victims awaiting
burial at Belsen concentration camp after liberation by
the British 2nd Army, who forced the German SS guards
to bury the corpses. Despite medical efforts, many more
died thereafter from irreversible disease and starvation.
Used by permission of Bettmann/CORBIS.

ings were removed from their teeth. Early on, the victims'
bodies were buried in mass graves, but by 1942 crematoria
were working full blast. Despite vigorous German efforts to
destroy evidence in the war's closing days, the Soviet army
found 368,820 men's suits, 836,255 women's coats and dresses,
large quantities of children's clothing and false teeth, and,
upon further searching in the tannery, seven tons of human
hair.

Lampshades, however, were probably not made from Jewish skin, nor soap from Jewish fat, despite persistent rumors—at least not in significant numbers. However, under the pressure of the Soviet advance, fat was rendered from the Jewish bodies in cremation to be poured back onto the flames and accelerate the burning. Jewish blood was extracted from seven hundred women at Auschwitz to be transfused to German soldiers, casting racial purity to the winds, and of course without concern for the women's survival; "the women were lying on the ground, faint, 'and deep rivers of blood were flowing around their bodies.' "[11]

Thousands of Jews' bodies were subjected to "experiments" (always conducted or supervised by physicians) that amounted to death by torture. This included freezing Jews to death to gain information to help downed German pilots; using a low-pressure chamber to simulate death by oxygen deprivation at high altitude (complete with "autopsies" performed while the "subject" was still alive); sterilization by X-ray; and many others. Twenty Jewish children were deliberately infected with tuberculosis for study and then murdered by hanging in April 1945 to remove the evidence. Some 3,000 twins, mostly children, were tortured in medical "experiments" by Dr. Josef Mengele with a wide variety of supposed scientific goals; 160 survived.

But much torture of the Jewish body was less systematic. One of the most moving of all Holocaust documents is the responsa—Rabbinic answers to practical questions of Jewish law—of Rabbi Ephraim Oshry of Kovno, Lithuania. Many questions had to do with the body, and they reveal as much about Jewish religious attitudes toward the body as they do about German cruelty.

A man the Germans had beaten deaf and dumb asked if he could be counted in a minyan—a prayer quorum. Although a deaf-mute is not strictly supposed to be counted, Rabbi Oshry ruled that he could and even be called to the Torah, if the deaf man concentrated on each word of the prayer while it was chanted by the reader. When the man read his ruling, his eyes brightened and he wrote, "Rabbi, you have revived me. May G-d console you and grant you life!"[12]

In one response, the rabbi ruled that a *kohein* whose testicles had been deliberately crushed—German police had caught him with a crust of bread hidden behind them to take to his starving family—could still be called to the Torah as the descendant of priests but could no longer have sex with his wife. In another, he found that a man who had had his left arm cut off for stealing food could have another man put tefillin on his right arm.

A man named Moshe Goldkorn repeatedly smuggled flour into the ghetto for Passover matzah: "Bit by bit, Goldkorn smuggled in enough flour to bake matzos for nearly 100 Jews, each of whom would receive one olive-sized piece of mat-zoh," the religiously prescribed minimum. Two days before Passover the Germans caught him with a small bag of flour and beat him savagely, breaking most of his teeth. Goldkorn posed his question in tears: " 'With my broken teeth, how can I fulfill the mitzvah of eating an olive-sized piece of *mat-zoh*?' " Didn't the law forbid eating soaked *matzoh*? But the rabbi ruled that this was "a stringency" beyond the law;

softening it in his mouth, Goldkorn ate his painfully smuggled *matzoh* "despite his wounds and his broken teeth."[13]

Rabbi Oshry also determined that if it was unavoidable, a Jew could eat in the presence of a corpse and that slave laborers could say the daily prayer thanking God "who has not made me a slave," because the freedom meant was not physical. However, the gold teeth of the dead could not be used for any reason.

Since pregnancy was punishable by death, he permitted contraception and abortion. But the very day the edict was put forth—May 8, 1942—a pregnant Jewish woman passed the ghetto hospital. A German soldier noticed her belly and shot her through the heart. Rabbi Oshry was nearby and was urgently asked if a Caesarean section was allowed. If the baby were dead, would it not be desecrating the mother's body? He ruled that the baby should be saved, but the meticulous Germans came to record the name of the murdered woman. One "grabbed the infant and cracked its skull against the wall of the hospital room."[14]

After the war, he encountered a woman who had been forced into sexual slavery and tattooed with PROSTITUTE for Hitler's soldiers. Could she live and sleep with her husband? Yes, but she should not remove the tattoo, despite the prohibition. "On the contrary, let her and her sisters preserve their tattoos and regard them not as signs of shame, but as signs of honor, pride, and courage—proof of what they suffered for the sanctification of G-d."[15] Likewise the most distinctive features of the late-twentieth-century Jewish body—the concentration camp numbers tattooed on the forearms of

Holocaust survivor #78501 lifts her glass of wine at a
Passover Seder in May 1986, celebrating the liberation of
the Hebrew slaves from Egypt.
Used by permission of Nathan Benn/CORBIS.

survivors. Oshry ruled that another woman should not
remove her number, "for by doing so she is fulfilling the
wishes of the accursed German evildoers and abetting their
effort to have the Holocaust forgotten."[16] During my childhood, the sight of those numbers on some older people's
arms was a source of disturbing fascination; the millions
whose gaze lingered on those chilling blue marks made them
links to a hideous recent past, helping ensure that neither
time nor denial will mount a successful "assault on truth and
memory."[17]

My friend Tosia, whose story comes next, is one of many
who say "Shoah," not "Holocaust." *Holocaust*—"completely
burnt"—refers to Temple sacrifices in Greek Bible translations. Holocaust implies that God wanted it, or worse, that

Jews were atoning for sins. Tosia is a survivor, and she says "Shoah"—catastrophe—with authority. But there is sacrifice in the idea of *Kiddush Hashem*, the sanctification of God's name, which applies to all who are killed because they are Jews. Because of familiarity, and so for memory's sake, I use both—or neither; really, it is a crime without a name.

9

Surviving

It is difficult to make the story told by the numbers come alive, even with many brief anecdotes. The numbers are numbing, and the anecdotes, taken out of an extended human context, seem almost beyond belief. That is why it is so important to read and hear the stories of the lives of individuals—both those who perished, like Anne Frank and Chana Senesh, and those who somehow made it out alive. And, of course, it is the survival stories that give us hope, that allow us to hear these dreadful tidings and go forward. With or without tattoos, they are written on the body.

Tosia Szechter Schneider is a gracious, good-humored lady with lively, shining eyes for whom these events are vivid and all too present.[1] They are also thoroughly embodied. One of her earliest memories is of refusing to kiss the hand of the Polish count her father worked for, but most are of play with friends—collecting chestnuts, sledding in the winter chill, swimming and splashing in the Dniester River in summer. One day before the war, she and her kindergarten classmates were "pelted with rocks by a group of Polish kids, shouting anti-Semitic slurs at us," but this event seemed marginal.

Tosia and her best friend, Genia, "wore Shirley Temple rings, played with cut-out dolls of Shirley Temple, and went to see her movies whenever we could get a few pennies together." They also played at war, in a deep ravine where some of the last war's dead were rumored to be buried. The girls were nurses, the boys heroic fighters. In winter she got frostbite because she loved to play in the snow.

She did chores like fetching wood for the stove, weeding and watering the garden, scrubbing the kitchen for the Sabbath, and storing food in the basement. "I liked to go down into the cellar on hot summer days and feel the cold damp walls." Before Passover, "Paste was applied to our burgundy colored floor, brushes were attached to our feet and then we danced around the room" until you could see your face in the polished floor.

She loved stories of the past. Her father fought for Austria and then for Poland; still, he had to scrub the Polish words OUT WITH THE JEWS from the wall of their home. There were stories of her mother's youth, "about the Cossacks burning, looting and raping women . . . how they had smeared my mother's face with charcoal, to make her look ugly, so the Cossacks would not be after her."

Just blossoming, Tosia had teenage crushes. On Saturday young people dressed up, "girls in groups, on one side of the road and the boys on the other. They would steal glances . . . whisper and giggle. In spring, as the lilac bloomed in our garden and bird songs were heard, the world seemed perfect and beautiful and so full of promise." Her father planted three peach trees, and in accordance with Leviticus 19—"you shall regard its fruit as its foreskin. Three years it shall be uncircumcised for you, not to be eaten"—they did not. War would come before they could.

But if war was in the air, so was the Zionist dream. When she visited her brother's summer camp, "There were tents erected, as far as the eye could see, and boys and girls in their blue and white uniforms strolled around. Blue and white Zionist flags fluttered in the breeze." Throughout Europe, Jewish youth were practicing pioneering, complete with muscle building, farming, and self-defense, but they were soon conscripted in Poland's feeble attempt to resist the Germans. In an opening action of the war, their town was bombed and the first Jewish child was killed. His father carried him to the cemetery where, in a paroxysm of grief, refusing help, he buried the boy.

Tosia's brother was forced to pave the German commandant's courtyard with Jewish tombstones from that cemetery. The Germans "dragged the rabbi out of his house, beat him mercilessly and demanded that he dance for them." Jews were strictly confined to their ghetto and doled out six hundred calories a day—part of a German mass starvation plan. Tosia saw "children with swollen stomachs begging in the streets." At night, lice brought torment and typhus.

She was also learning something new about her body. Mueller, her father's uniformed supervisor, showed up at their door one night:

He sat down, took off his holster and gun and started talking with my parents. He seemed a bit drunk and my parents were terrified because a German was not allowed to socialize with Jews. . . . [H]e became more aggressive and . . . I saw him standing over my bed, mumbling something in German. . . . I was told later, that he called me "my blond angel." He then went into the kitchen, put a gun to my mother's head and demanded that she confess that "bei dieser ist ein Arier gewesen" (that an Aryan had fathered this one). My brother sneaked me out of the house.

Despite German efficiency, there was much taunting and torture. "Orthodox Jews had their side locks ripped off, many people were beaten and some were shot." But, ordered to wear identifying armbands, "girls embroidered the Star of David armbands for their boyfriends and romances flourished." She could still feel angry when the Germans took her beloved fur muff and the fur collar from her winter coat.

During a roundup billed as a group inoculation, Tosia's family sneaked back into their old house and lay on the cold kitchen floor. "At night, as my parents, my brother and I lay huddled together," a Ukrainian man "entered the kitchen and covered us all with a sheepskin coat. This simple act of compassion brought tears to my eyes." Meanwhile hundreds were crammed into the synagogue awaiting "inoculation." "One woman tried to come closer to the door to help her fainting baby get a breath of air, but a German soldier grabbed the baby from the mother's arms and smashed its head on the Holy Ark and then shot the mother."

In this one action, "Half of the town's Jewish population, 2,500 men, women and children," were driven seven miles to the Dniester River, where Tosia had played. One wounded woman made it back and related that "they were forced to undress in a barn and then run in groups of five to an open pit where they were shot. . . . As music was blaring . . . and vodka was flowing, the Germans and their helpers took turns shooting." During the roundup the Germans entered a Jewish orphanage, "smashed some of the babies' heads on the walls and threw others from the second floor into the street, where a truck collected them."

In the second roundup, Tosia lost her best friend, Genia, thirteen, who had "brown eyes and lovely brown curls," and her cousin Wisia, nineteen. "She was a pretty girl of small build, with dark curly hair . . . and was a very gifted dress designer. I watched . . . as she made lovely flowers out of velvet and different scraps of material for the cotillion ball at the gymnasium. She also liked to comb my long hair and arranged it like a crown on my head."

Her father gave each family member a poison pill to use as a last resort. They fled to another ghetto, but nothing changed. After her father's murder, her mother starved while giving her ration to her children. Going for water one day, Tosia was seen by a Ukrainian policeman, who said "he did not want to see any filthy Jews. He slapped me in the face and told me to run. As I ran up the hill, I heard shots being fired but they missed me."

Her mother somehow procured Aryan papers for her and walked her to the ghetto's edge. Tosia had already removed her armband when she decided she could not leave her mother and brother. She was fourteen years old. Her blond hair and Aryan looks brought other chances, but she rejected them.

Her mother died of typhus at thirty-nine; her last words to her crying daughter were in Yiddish: "*du virst noch glicklich zayn mayn kind*"—"you will still be happy, my child." Tosia had typhus, too; she was feverish and barely conscious when her brother and cousins wrapped their mother in a sheet, laid her gently on the floor according to Jewish custom, found a candle, and said the Mourner's Kaddish. "The flame of the candle at her side danced before my eyes, and then all went dark for a very long time." Her brother buried her in the dead of night in what was left of the Jewish cemetery.

She and her brother fled to a work camp, but after a shooting action there, she and her friends "began to collect our fallen comrades. . . . Seventeen young boys and girls had been murdered on that day. Among them was my brother Julek, not quite eighteen." A few days later she stopped by the mass grave she had helped dig. "The Ukrainian guard screamed at me to return to work and then proceeded to urinate on the grave."

She took the great risk of seeking a friend of her father's in a village six miles away. She bartered her clothes for a peasant's outfit and walked barefoot, stopping to kneel and cross herself at wayside shrines to reduce suspicion. She talked her way through a roadblock. But the friend, who used to dandle her on his knee and say that her father had saved his life, would not help her, even refusing her a pair of old shoes for her bleeding feet. When on the road back she happened upon two weeping Jewish girls who had been raped, she wondered how to weigh this crime with murder all around them.

After the liberation, very gradually, "The wounds on my legs and arms healed, my gums stopped bleeding, but I was still continuously hungry, no matter how much I ate. . . . I often woke up screaming at night, a recurring dream of being captured by the Germans. This lasted for many years and still happens, occasionally." VE Day brought dancing in the streets, but Tosia was mourning. "There was life all around me but I felt dead inside."

Returning home, she and other Jews found their Polish neighbors not glad to see them; the only good thing the Germans had done, they said, was to kill the Jews. Those who had saved Jews hid the fact from others. Later, in Germany, no one admitted to having supported the Nazis. Denazification seemed a farce, but she had to see some kind of punishment and got a pass to the Nuremberg trials: "When I faced Göring and all the other top Nazis . . . I felt a deep hatred, loathing and revulsion looking at those totally unremarkable ugly faces. Were these the faces of evil?"

Most were never tried. Whenever Tosia saw a German of military age, she thought of him shooting her brother. She studied Hebrew, planning to go to Israel, but the British blocked her and she came to America, where she found a telegram from a brilliant and kind young man who had tutored her in Germany after the war. Today she is alive and well and married to him sixty years later. Visits from grandchildren are probably more frequent than nightmares.

But her body remembers: when it was filthy and stinking from being condemned to inhuman squalor, fevered and skeletal from deliberately inflicted typhus and starvation, gums gushing blood on biting a crust of bread, the relentless gnaw of hunger in her belly, her hands and feet shredded and bleeding from forced marches and slave labor, and her heart broken again and again by murder upon murder of everyone she loved.

Only yesterday. One Jewish body among millions; and, she would hasten to tell you, one of the lucky ones.

10

The Body Returns

Some have thought that if the Diaspora had not physically enervated and pacified the Jews, they might have been more difficult targets of mass murder. Certainly many Holocaust victims must have longed for the return of the Hebrew warriors of old who might have defended and protected them. But Jewish ambivalence about physical strength is evident even in the Bible. "There were giants in the earth in those days," says Genesis, at least in the King James Version, and even the standard Jewish translation says, "when the divine beings cohabited with the daughters of men, who bore them offspring. They were the heroes of old, the men of renown" (Gen. 6:4). But they or their descendants became wicked and were destroyed by the Flood. Goliath, another giant whose superhuman strength availed him little, was felled by a clever slip of a boy with a slingshot and, of course, God on his side. Samson was a Nazarite, whose vows to God made him a sort of super-Jew with magical strength that he used against the enemies of the Jews, but he . . . well, we know what happened to him. So much for the value of bodily power in and of itself.

Samson, blinded, brings down the Philistines' temple on their
heads, dying as both victor and victim, punished for forgetting
that his strength came from God.
Woodcut illustration by Julius Schnorr von Carolsfeld.

But there is another side to the biblical view. Jacob wrestles successfully with an unearthly being, possibly God
himself, and gets a new name—*Isra-el*, or God-wrestler.
David, that slip of a boy gathering stones, fought lions and
bears with his hands to protect his sheep. Although when
King Saul is seeking his life, David comes upon him in a deep
sleep and, instead of killing Saul, cuts off a piece of his garment to prove that he easily could have; the boy grows up to
be a mighty warrior. (The Israelites' chant, "Saul has slain
his thousands, David his ten thousands," does not endear

David to the King.) And there are the Maccabees, postbiblical heroes who, through a blend of strength and godliness, overthrow an idolatrous, tyrannical regime in a war where the odds are hugely against them.

Even some of the great early Rabbis were known for their physical strength, as others were for their sexual passion or beauty. Rabbi Amram, we saw, combined two of these when he moved an impossibly heavy ladder so he could climb up to some women. Resh Lakish was transformed from a champion gladiator into a sage when he spied Rabbi Yohanan bathing in the Jordan and jumped in after him with something more like Greek than Jewish intent. The Rabbi tells him his strength should be for the Torah, but he only replies that Yohanan's beauty should be for women. The Rabbi offers Resh Lakish his sister, "more beautiful than I," in exchange for repentance and study. It's a deal: "He taught him Bible and Mishnah, and made him into a great man."[1]

Later there is a tiff; in a debate about the ritual purity of knives and spears, the teacher rather tastelessly reminds the pupil about his past: "A robber understands about robbery." But Resh (an acronym for "Rabbi Shimon") replies tartly, "What good have you done me? There they called me Master, and here they call me Master," as if to say, *I'm as much a master scholar as you, but I was a master gladiator before I ever met you.*

And even after this, in a sort of last hurrah for the Jews of ancient Israel, they rebelled against the Roman emperor Hadrian, who—echoing the Greeks of three centuries earlier—planned to rebuild the Temple as a shrine to himself and forbade all Jewish practices on pain of death. Simeon Bar Kochba, "Son of a Star," was their hero, and no less a figure than the great Rabbi Akiva, aging, weak, and desperate for a shred of hope, thought he was the Messiah. He quoted Numbers 24:17, "The star hath trodden forth out of Jacob," and referred to the new champion as "the Messianic king."[2] Coming just sixty years after the second destruction of Jerusalem, this heady mix of political revolt and end-times passion swept through the despairing Jews like brushfire.

Rome annihilated them. Hundreds of thousands were slaughtered; children were dragged from school and enslaved. One observer wrote, " 'Why are you being taken to execution?' 'Because I circumcised my son.' 'Why are you being taken to crucifixion?' 'Because I read the Torah.' " Akiva, once the most handsome and forceful of sages, languished in a Roman jail, a frail old man still trying to teach the forbidden faith through the bars. His execution echoes annually across nineteen centuries in a text read on Yom Kippur, the holiest day of the Jewish year. His flesh was flayed from his body with red-hot iron combs. His last words were the Shema, "Hear O Israel, the Lord is our God, the Lord is . . ." and with his last breath he made the essential Jewish declaration, "One." Jews who go to synagogue only once a year on the Day of Atonement are thus exposed to this anguished martyrology, as close as Judaism gets to the physical mortification of Christ. But the lessons Jews took from this chastisement were very different.

This open rebellion was no path to salvation, but the last gasp of Jewish life in ancient Israel. After such catastrophic failure, Jewish resistance became quiet and spiritual. Throughout Diaspora history, scholarship counted far more than strength, and study was the acknowledged key to godliness. There were exceptions. Shmuel Ha-Nagid—Samuel the Prince—was a great warrior of Muslim Spain in charge of the Armies of Granada, and some of the Jews of India secured their high status through military exploits on behalf of local rulers. Wherever Jews were allowed to join the army, they did, and they fought for the countries they lived in. But for the most part the mighty Jewish heroes of bodily prowess and battlefield skill belonged to a lost, ancient, almost mythic time.

Or else, to the realm of fantasy. One of the stranger legends in Jewish folklore is that of the golem, a sort of benign Frankenstein monster created by a Rabbi to protect the Jews of Prague. The word appears once in the Bible, in Psalm 139, as a reference to the unformed limbs of the supplicant seeking help from God, and in the Talmud it is used to describe Adam after he has been shaped from dust but before God breathes the breath of life into his body. So, too, the Rabbis of legend could, with God's help, bring a golem to life. In the Prague version, the Rabbi makes it from clay and brings it to life by writing the word *emet*—"truth"—on its forehead. But as monsters will, the golem grows bigger and stronger, threatening those it was created to protect. By erasing the aleph, the first letter of *emet*, the Rabbi leaves only *met*, death, and the golem's life is done.

The golem shows one side of the Jewish relationship to physical strength: You can get it only by building something alien—not human and certainly not Jewish. You use the power of literacy in the holy tongue to control the creature's life and death, and you have such power only if a lifetime of bookish study has made you a great sage. As in the Bible, strength comes from teaming up with God.

But from the mid-nineteenth century, Jews in Europe became a bit obsessed with Jewish "softness" and developed theories about how to change the Jewish body through physical labor, activity, and sports. Ironically, one of the signature calls for this transformation came from a young Sephardic Jewish woman in New York:

> What we need to-day, second only to the necessity of closer union and warmer patriotism, is the building up of our national, physical force. If the new Ezra rose to lead our people to a secure house of refuge, whence would he recruit the farmers, masons, carpenters, artisans, competent to perform the arduous, practical pioneer work of founding a new nation? We read of the Jews who attempted to rebuild the Temple using the trowel with one hand, while with the other they warded off the blows of the molesting enemy. Where are the warrior-mechanics today equal to either feat. . . . For nineteen hundred years we have been living on an idea; our spirit has been abundantly fed, but our body has been starved.

She imagined and believed in the vision of a new yet ancient kind of Jew, of the sort described in the book of Nehemiah (4:17–18) rebuilding the city wall of Jerusalem. In the King James Version she would have known well,

> They which builded on the wall, and they that bare burdens, with those that laded, every one with one of his hands wrought in the work, and with the other hand held a weapon.
>
> For the builders, every one had his sword girded by his side, and so builded. And he that sounded the trumpet was by me.

She went on literally to flesh out her vision:

> Let our first care to-day be the re-establishment of our physical strength, the reconstruction of our national organism, so that in future, where the respect due to us cannot be won by entreaty, it may be commanded, and where it cannot be commanded, it may be enforced.[3]

This is from an article serialized in 1882 in *American Hebrew*, a magazine widely ready by American Jews. It was a year before she wrote the poem that made her famous, pulled out of a pile in a contest judged by Ralph Waldo Emerson, and now carved in bronze at the base of the Statue of Liberty. She was Emma Lazarus.

"Give me your tired, your poor, your huddled masses yearning to breathe free, the wretched refuse of your teeming shore" were the words she put in the mouth of the giant statue, a sort of golem-mother of exiles, "a mighty woman with a torch" who could shelter an almost endless stream of sufferers. And the truth she gave this bronze near-goddess to speak helped awaken her to life in the minds of millions. These words aroused compassion for all oppressed people who yearned toward America's gates. Lazarus felt their anguish and sympathized with their dreams. But she also felt the special situation of her own people everywhere.

> Our adversaries are perpetually throwing dust in our eyes with the accusations of materialism and tribalism, and we . . . fall into the trap they set. . . . "Tribal!" This perpetual taunt rings so persistently in our ears . . . in face of the fact that our "tribal God" has become the God of two thirds of the inhabited globe . . . and that as a people we have adapted ourselves to the varying customs and climates of every nation in the world . . . our national defect is that we are not "tribal" enough; we have not sufficient solidarity to perceive that when the life and property of a Jew in the uttermost provinces of the Caucasus are attacked, the dignity of a Jew in free America is humiliated.

This serial "Epistle to the Hebrews," with its ringing cry for Jewish solidarity, came in the wake of rising anti-Semitism and pogroms in Russia and elsewhere in Europe.

But it also came just at the moment when the first modern settlements of European Jews were being established in Israel. This would be known as the First Aliyah, or "going

A despairing Diaspora Jew, unaware of a Jewish angel pointing him
toward the Zionist dream of healthy physical labor on the land,
in the sun. Designed by E. M. Lilien for the Zionist Congress of
1901. At the top: "The Fifth Zionist Congress in Basel," with the
Hebrew date; at the bottom: "And may our eyes see Your return
to Zion in mercy," part of one of the holiest prayers said
three times daily by religious Jews.
*By permission of the I. Edward Kiev Collection, Gelman Library,
George Washington University.*

up," the term for Jewish migration to Israel, and in less than
a decade it doubled the population of Jews to about fifty
thousand. The year of the first Lazarus article, 1882, was also
the birth year of the first child to grow up speaking modern
Hebrew. Jews throughout the world had begun to think a
return to Zion was possible.

But these were not the devout Jews drawn to Jerusalem in

a steady trickle throughout history, come to kiss the sacred stones of the old city, to thread their way through old Arab alleyways to find a bit of the Wailing Wall, pray, weep, and with mincing steps wend their way home again. These settlers had a new ideology, at its heart the same two declarations that animated Emma: Jews must help one another survive; and Jews must go back to the land, perform redemptive physical labor, build up their strength, and raise their hands in their own defense—so that in the future, "*where the respect due to us cannot be won by entreaty, it may be commanded, and where it cannot be commanded, it may be enforced.*"

It was not just a means to an end, even as vital an end as survival. It was an article of secular faith, a belief that centuries of confinement, deprivation, and oppression, centuries of books and handicrafts and money, and centuries of legalistic spirituality had robbed the Jewish body of its native strength, and that Jews would never be able to raise their heads high among nations and peoples until this strength was regained. These Jews looked back to Joshua, Deborah, David, and Judah Maccabee not with religious fervor and wistful bookish longing but with a gritty conviction that the physical strength and warrior spirit of the Jews was real and would be real again. They looked up to Theodor Herzl, the great Zionist leader whose physically imposing size, poise, and charisma—as different from the average Jew as a European prince—made him seem like the Messiah. And they looked forward to the Jews of the future, farmers, builders, fighters, lovers, redeeming Jewish honor *with their bodies.*

One Zionist thinker behind this dogma of the body was Max Nordau,[4] a physician, journalist, and philosopher whose father was a rabbi. "When I reached the age of fifteen," he wrote, "I left the Jewish way of life and the study of the Torah. . . . Judaism remained a mere memory and since then I have always felt as a German and as a German only."[5] The year of his departure would have been 1864, but by the mid-1890s Nordau, like his friend Herzl, was disabused of his dream of assimilation by the Dreyfus trial, in which a decorated French officer who was Jewish was wrongly accused of and punished for treason later proved to have been committed by others. This occurred in the context of vicious anti-Semitism—"Death to the Jews!" was the rallying cry. In time it would be fulfilled in France and throughout Europe, but for now it gave Zionism the impetus it needed.

Nordau's role, apart from being one of Herzl's greatest supporters, was to imagine the new Jewish body. His medical thinking led him to see neurasthenia—nervous weakness— as the illness of the modern age, one that eventually led to degeneration and hysteria. He blamed it for what he saw as the degeneracy of modern art. While anti-Semitism, especially the increasingly virulent racist variety, was one of the signs of this ailment, Nordau did not exempt the Jews from the diagnosis. Nor, for that matter, did other turn-of-the-century physicians, Jewish or not; indeed they saw neurasthenia as characteristic of Jews.

But Nordau had what was for him a decisive answer to the

general ill health and even the racial inferiority of the Jews. He called it *Muskeljudentum*—"muscle-Jewry"—and it became one of the most debated ideas about the Jews. He first proposed it at the Second Zionist Congress of 1898 in Basel, Switzerland, saying, "We must think of creating once again a Jewry of muscles."[6] He went on to write an article called "Muskeljudentum" in a prominent Jewish journal in June 1903, reminding readers that

> history is our witness that such a Jewry had once existed.
>
> For too long, all too long have we been engaged in the mortification of our own flesh.
>
> Or rather, to put it more precisely—others did the killing for us. Their extraordinary success is measured by hundreds of thousands of Jewish corpses in the ghettos, in the churchyards, along the highways of medieval Europe. . . . We would have preferred to develop our bodies rather than to kill them or to have them—figuratively and literally—killed by others.

This was four decades before the gas chambers. But in Nordau's view the physical conditions of the Jews, the very elements they lived in, had conspired against their bodies for centuries:

> All the elements of Aristotelian physics—light, air, water, and earth—were measured out to us very sparingly. In the narrow Jewish street our poor limbs soon forgot their gay movements; in the dimness of sunless

houses our eyes began to blink shyly; the fear of constant persecution turned our powerful voices into frightened whispers, which rose in crescendo only when our martyrs on the stakes cried out their dying prayers in the face of their executioners. But now, all coercion has become a memory of the past, and at least we are allowed space enough for our bodies to live again. Let us take up our oldest traditions; let us once more become deep-chested, sturdy, sharp-eyed men.

Although he had medical authority, in some ways Nordau seemed to be playing into anti-Semitic hands. At Chanukah in 1907, the Menorah Society at Harvard was addressed by that university's most distinguished president, Charles Eliot, who told the assembled Jews that their people "are distinctly inferior in stature and physical development . . . to any other race." He bemoaned the lack of Maccabean martial spirit and recommended they join the militia. Despite the respectful reference to the Maccabees, this was polite-society anti-Semitism, circa 1907.

But whether or not he echoed anti-Semites, Dr. Nordau intended literally to remake the Jewish body, and it was a message many Jews were ready for. At the Basel conference, he and his fellow physician Max Mandelstamm proposed a network of gymnastics clubs to enhance the physical fitness of Jewish youth. They called these Bar Kochba clubs, after the hero of the second revolt against Rome, or Maccabi clubs, recalling the warrior-champions of the Chanukah story. Within a few years these clubs had spread throughout

The Bar Kochba Jewish Athletic Club of Berlin, 1902,
part of a network of clubs inspired by Max Nordau's
idea of "muscle-Jewry."
Bildarchiv Preussischer Kulturbesitz / Art Resources, NY. Used by permission.

the European Jewish world, and Nordau's essay would
spread them further:

> For no other people will gymnastics fulfill a more edu-
> cational purpose than for us Jews. It shall straighten us
> in body and in character. It shall give us self-

confidence, although our enemies maintain that we already have too much self-confidence as it is. But who knows better than we do that their imputations are wrong. We completely lack a sober confidence in our physical prowess.

Our new muscle-Jews have not yet regained the heroism of our forefathers who in large numbers eagerly entered the sports arenas in order to take part in competition and to pit themselves against the highly trained Hellenistic athletes and the powerful Nordic barbarians. But morally, even now the new muscle-Jews surpass their ancestors, for the ancient Jewish circus fighters were ashamed of their Judaism and tried to conceal the sign of the Covenant by means of a surgical operation . . . while the members of the "Bar Kochba" club loudly and proudly affirm their national loyalty.

Nordau called for a Greek ideal for Jews. He was a loyal Zionist, but as Herzl noted in his diary,[7] they had at first very different concepts of the time frame:

November 19, 1895

Nordau, it would seem, is completely won over to the cause. My talk with him concerns objections in the higher realms; "If the Jews are anthropologically fit for nationhood?"—and the like.

Experience will tell.

Nordau thinks that the plan will need three hundred years for its realization.

I believe thirty—provided the idea makes headway.

A few years later, Yosef Yekutieli, a fifteen-year-old inspired by the 1912 Olympics in Stockholm, conceived the idea for a Jewish international equivalent. In 1932, his dream was realized, and the first Maccabiah Games were held. They were named for Judah Maccabee, and the year marked exactly eighteen centuries from the Bar Kochba rebellion. Eighteen is an auspicious number for Jews, since the letters of the word *chai*, meaning life, have that numerical value. At this writing, the eighteenth Maccabiah Games will soon be held in Tel Aviv, a large metropolis that was not even a village when Nordau penned his manifesto. At least seven thousand Jewish athletes from sixty countries will compete—in terms of participants, one of the five largest sporting events in the world. Three hundred years to change the Jewish body, to prepare it "anthropologically" for nationhood. Three hundred years to build confidence by building muscle and bone. Three hundred years to make the Jews *comfortable* in their bodies for the first time since ancient Rome. It would not be merely historic change, it would be biological evolution. But Herzl's impatient dream proved to be more real. Just two years later, on September 3, 1897, on arriving back home in Vienna from the First Zionist Congress, Herzl wrote that "our movement has entered the stream of history.

> If I were to sum up the Congress in a word—which I shall take care not to publish—it would be this: At Basel I founded the Jewish State.
>
> If I said this out loud today I would be greeted by

The dreamer Herzl on a hotel balcony in Basel,
Switzerland, during the First World
Zionist Congress in 1897.
Used by permission of Getty Images.

universal laughter. In five years perhaps, and certainly
in fifty years, everyone will perceive it.[8]

Exactly fifty years and eighty-seven days later, on November 29, 1947, the United Nations voted to end the British
Mandate and partition its territory into a Jewish and an
Arab state; Israel's nationhood was proclaimed on May 14
the following year.

But Nordau's glacial time frame was proven wrong before
the ink was dry on his "Muskeljudentum"; it was not evolu-

tion, it was revolution. Just as the First Aliyah was under way when Emma Lazarus's "Epistle to the Jews" was published, so the Second Aliyah gained momentum just after Nordau's essay came out. Between 1904 and 1914, an estimated forty thousand Jews came to Israel, mainly from Russia. One of them, Aaron David Gordon, was a leading theorist of Socialist Zionism, a critical strand of the Second Aliyah, and was a founder of the first kibbutz, Degania.

Although a forty-eight-year-old intellectual when he came to Israel, Gordon had a Tolstoyan reverence for farming and farmers—Tolstoy, like the Zionists, believed in the redemptive power of working the land—and Gordon labored in the fields alongside much younger men and women. He inspired them. A major part of the Jewish "problem" was that Jews were rarely allowed to own land, which led to an "unhealthy" alienation from physical labor on the soil. At his death in 1922, Gordon was widely known in Israel as an old man with a long white beard who farmed in the fields of the kibbutz all day and led the young men and women in song and dance at night.

But all was not song, dance, and working the soil. Causes of death ranged from malaria to suicide; there were Arab attacks, and Jews in the older settlements had hired Bedouin and Arab guards—basically a protection racket in which the Jews paid Arabs not to attack them. Second Aliyah immigrants had been involved in Jewish defense groups in Russia and found this extortion reprehensible. In 1907, a group of ten Jews began to protect a settlement themselves, and their success led to an expanded multisettlement organization called Ha-Shomer—the Guard. They dressed as Arabs and spoke Arabic well but slung bandoliers of bullets across their chests like Mexican revolutionaries. They were good horsemen, considered both fierce and fair by the Bedouin, and their motto said it all: "*By blood and fire Judah fell, by blood and fire Judah will rise up.*"

This was a new and different muscle-Jew. To Nordau's club gymnastics and Gordon's brawny grappling with the soil, Ha-Shomer and its descendants added self-defense. These proud and slightly wild defenders of their people gave life at last to the words of Emma Lazarus thirty years earlier: *Where the respect due to us cannot be won by entreaty, it may be commanded, and where it cannot be commanded, it may be enforced.* These first real enforcers of Jewish safety in eighteen centuries would have thrilled her, but their commitment to violence was not without controversy. An organization with a similar name formed in Vienna—Ha-Shomer Ha-Tza'ir, the Young Guard—and in 1917, they issued an ideological broadside that melded with other streams of Jewish thought. They verged on the anti-Semitic.

We are not complete and healthy men, and we are not complete and healthy Jews; we lack the harmony which should reign between these two fundamental elements of the "I" in us. . . .

Let us look closely at the Jewish youth. Even before he is twenty he is an old man. His soul is shrouded in deep darkness. . . .

Where is the optimism that makes life worth living,

that gives strength to bear the sufferings of life and that gives the young man encouragement, joy, and vigor? . . .

This and more. In addition to youth, we lack also a pure and true humanity. We stand, therefore, as the miserable inheritors of the faults of our fathers. And these faults are numerous and evil.[9]

Aside from breaking the fifth commandment and brimming with self-loathing, these words could hardly have been distressing to the enemies of the Jews. They attribute their critique to high objectives: "Our love for our people is strong and loyal. We wish to see our nation great and noble." Still, "The average Jew is but a caricature of a man healthy and normal in body and soul."

How can we become young and healthy? . . . The young and most extreme coined the phrase: "Let us give up the books and grasp the sword!" Only the first part of this slogan is acceptable to us. We agree, in fact we strive, for an end to the idolatrous worship of books which is typical of us. Everything we say or write or think gives off the odor of mold on worn-out pages. . . . But must the need to abandon books lead inevitably . . . to the sword? We think that there is yet another way—that is, in becoming closer to nature . . . we hope that nature will return to us the freshness, the optimism, the love of beauty characteristic of youth, that it will straighten our crooked back, stretch our muscles and strengthen our resolve.

Yet even as they excoriate musty books, they claim that

> for us the Bible stands above all; we wish to make it our
> primer . . . to remain young Hebrews. Our ideal is of a
> young Jew of strong body and courageous spirit, whose
> thoughts are healthy and normal, not hair-splitting
> and sophistic, who is disciplined and knows how to
> obey, a Jew to the depths of his heart . . . he loves all
> that is beautiful and noble. We will form a group of
> such youths—and Zion will be built!

But in the end the sword—in fact, the gun—was crucial
in rebuilding Zion, and history confirmed the virile image of
the "warrior-mechanics" invoked by Lazarus, "the Jews who
attempted to rebuild the Temple using the trowel with one
hand, while with the other they warded off the blows of the
molesting enemy." The young Austrian Zionists could say
what they liked from the safety of Vienna, but the ones in
Israel did not have the luxury of rejecting the sword. And
unlike the boys in Vienna, they did not see themselves nobly
blending into nature for spiritual renewal. They were not in
the lush Austrian countryside. Nature for them meant rocks,
sand, swamps, and pestilence. They needed to *dominate*
nature and they did.

Remarkably for the era, this strong-armed return to soil
and sword was not just for men. Socialist Zionism promoted
gender equality at least in theory, and women took their
places side by side with men in the fields and orchards and
even on the front lines of defense. That was the reason
behind the controversial children's house that characterized

David Ben-Gurion: Russian immigrant, attorney,
member of the Jewish Legion of the British Army that
fought the Turks in World War I, and later the first
Prime Minister of Israel. He proclaimed the birth
of the Jewish state on May 14, 1948.
Used by permission of Bettmann/CORBIS.

kibbutz child-rearing for the first two-thirds of the twentieth century. Children would be raised mainly in group settings with caregivers outside the family and would even
sleep in those settings, not just to give children a truly communal identity but also so women could work on an equal
footing with men.

This was not easily achieved. One kibbutz had been

founded by East European Jews in the early twenties in a malarial swamp and by the early fifties had five hundred members.[10] Another was settled by forty-nine people in 1938 as an outpost to defend the border with Lebanon; by 1970, it had over four hundred members. Despite theoretical equality, leaders were typically men. Still, "women superficially strived to take on men's roles. They dressed in baggy shorts, refused to wear make-up, and prided themselves on physical strength."[11] Yet they were not considered to be strong enough to do everything men did: "The pioneer-settler ethos of the kibbutz movement was predicated on masculine norms of physical power and aggressiveness."[12] Egalitarian or not, this ideology of "physical power and aggressiveness" was clear.

Members of agricultural settlements in Israel supplied the leadership of the defense organizations and army units. As the strong young settlers of the early twentieth century had formed the Jewish Legion to help the British fight the Turks, those of mid-century formed the Jewish Brigade to help them fight the Germans.[13] Five thousand enlisted in three battalions. They had defended their farms against Arab raiders for decades, but now they were equipped and trained to fight the German army. They painted their artillery shells with a makeshift Jewish star and, in Hebrew, the words *Shay l'Hitler*—"A Gift for Hitler."[14] They assaulted well-fortified German positions and engaged in hand-to-hand combat with bayonets. During one assault a certain Corporal Levy stood on a German bunker, shouting, "*Heraus ihr schweine, die Juden sind da!*"—"*Get out you pigs, the Jews are here!*" They visited Mauthausen concentration camp, where one barely surviving inmate pointed at the Star of David on one of their uniforms and asked in all sincerity, "You're Jewish angels?"[15] After the armistice, disobeying orders, they brought many survivors to Israel, and many of those in turn became farmers.

A kibbutz founded in 1928, in the Jezreel Valley by seventeen Tel Aviv Israelis—they had previously tried and failed in a malarial swamp—bracketed this period. It was the subject of an oral history in the late seventies, after many changes.[16] Yehuda, the only founder then still alive, had been born in Russia in 1909. During World War I, his town had been burned by Russian soldiers to keep it from the Germans; his family had to wander in the forest but at last made it to Israel. At first the kibbutz had many dropouts and three suicides.

"We set out to create a fundamental revolution in our lives, both as Jews and as human beings," Yehuda said. "We succeeded more or less in doing this. As in life, there is the dream and there is reality. . . . We did manage to create such a society in our lifetime . . . the whole kibbutz movement has achieved more than anyone thought or expected. There are, however, questions from within, and anxiety is our constant companion."

He was most troubled by the trend toward hired labor, which he saw as undermining the fundamental ideology: "I see manual work, physical labor, as one of our basic principles. . . . This is the Jewish problem: all of the traditional Jewish occupations! And this was our revolution: we wanted to send roots into the soil! And then you see someone, who for twenty or thirty years worked productively . . . suddenly showing his other nature, that of the Diaspora Jew, looking for easy ways of making money, becoming a merchant. We haven't changed his basic identity as much as we thought we had. This is what I am fighting against."[17]

An almost anti-Semitic note is struck here, by a Jew who has earned the right to champion physical labor but not the right to make racial generalizations. Muscle-Jews made Israel a nation again, but where would they have been without Eliezer Ben-Yehuda, the bookish linguist who insisted on speaking to his dog and his mother in Hebrew (neither understood him), and by sheer force of *mind* created modern Hebrew? Or without Herzl, that European dandy and inveterate talker and scribbler who never moved to Israel and never got dirt under his fingernails except for ink but who happened to scribble *The Jewish State*, a little book that changed history? Or Chaim Weizmann, whose hands smelled not of soil but of laboratory chemicals, yet whose studious tinkering helped save England in World War I and who therefore could persuade Lord Balfour to proclaim the British government's promise of a Jewish homeland in Israel? Or Albert Einstein, a luftmensch if ever there was one, who lent the full force of his huge international reputation (another airy thing) to persuade an American president to build the atomic bomb before the Germans did and then to help bring the Jewish state into being?

Still, it was the mostly anonymous muscle-Jews who did the work on and in the ground. *Muscle-Jews* wrested perma-

Romanian poster for a 1930s film about Zionism and life
in Israel, for recruitment and fund-raising.
Courtesy of the Central Zionist Archives, Jerusalem.
Used by permission of Rochelle Rubenstein of the CAR.

nently productive farms from swamps and sand. *They* fought
off Arab marauders and died with their love for the land in
their hearts and on their lips. *They* supplied the leadership of
the army, the people, and the state for three generations.
They sustained six thousand deaths—1 percent of the Jewish
population, or the equivalent of three million Americans—

in the war for Israel's independence. *They* fought off six invading Arab armies in that war and two others. *They* destroyed the Syrian and Egyptian air forces pointed at Israel's heart and the weapons-grade nuclear reactor being built by Saddam Hussein in Iraq. Without mind, to be sure, but also without muscle, there would have been no Israel.

11

Tough Jews

Nordau may not have known it, but by the time he was exhorting Jews to hone their bodies, some Jews an ocean away had done that for generations and used those bodies not just in gymnastics but in fighting. Jews fought for their country, sometimes heroically, and often died in the American Revolution, the Mexican War, and on both sides in the Civil War, among others, and would also fight, proportional to their numbers, in both World Wars to come. In addition, by the turn of the twentieth century, American Jews were fighting for glory in the boxing ring and for ignominy if not a certain grudging fame on the streets of America's major cities.

In fact, by Nordau's time, just across the North Sea in England, there had already been muscle-Jews for at least a century, not common but prominent and important to the self-image of the weaker Jews around them.[1] One was the famous Daniel Mendoza, a prizefighter in late-eighteenth-century London. Sephardic, like most English Jews at the time, he was called "Mendoza the Jew" and "The Light of Israel." Boxing was bare-fisted, no holds or blows were

Prizefighter Daniel Mendoza (*far left*), "The Light of
Israel," 1790. Five-foot-seven and tipping the scales at
160 pounds, Mendoza dominated English boxing for
years and wrote *The Art of Boxing.* Benny Leonard
(*far right*), one of the great lightweight fighters
of all time, in November 1925.
*Photo by Topical Press Agency/Stringer. Collection: Hulton Archive.
Used by permission of Getty Images.*

barred, and there were no weight classes, but 160-pound
Mendoza regularly beat men 40 or 50 pounds heavier than he
was, becoming Champion of the London Prize Ring and
inspiring the Jews of England.

Mendoza fought neighborhood bullies, defending his mistress from anti-Semitic slurs, but (*mind* again) he was known
as the first "scientific" boxer, inventing the jabs, sparring,

and footwork that have been staples ever since. He wrote *The Art of Boxing*, which helped professionalize the sport. He became the darling of the Jews of the East End and a model for others: Sam Elias ("The Terrible Jew") weighed 130 pounds but often won, claiming to drink three glasses of gin a day while training. He may have invented the uppercut, a boon to a small man. There were Barney Aaron, "The Star of the East," Barnard Levy, Solomon Sodicky, and many others.

But with the migration of two million mostly poor Jews, boxing's center moved across the Atlantic, and Jewish fighters thrived. One said, "In San Francisco ya learned to use your left hook as part of your bar mitzvah instructions." They became superb defensive fighters to avoid getting their faces bruised, which would alert their Orthodox parents to what they were doing.

There were hundreds in the five or six decades bracketing the turn of the century—Jackie "Kid" Berg (Judah Bergman), "Corporal" Izzy Schwartz, Al Singer "The Bronx Beauty," Leach Cross (Louis Wallach) "The Fighting Dentist," Solly Krieger, and Maxie "Slapsie" Rosenbloom, to name a few. There were *forty* Jewish world championships. Benny Leonard (Benjamin Leiner), one of the best loved, held the World Lightweight Championship. Jackie Fields (Yonkel Finkelstein) became the youngest Olympic Gold Medal Winner and World Welterweight Champion twice. Mushy Callahan (Moishele Sheer), Al McCoy (Alex Rudolph), and Jack Bernstein were other champions. Victor Perez, a 110-pound Tunisian Jew, was flyweight champion of the world; deported to Auschwitz from France in 1943, he was forced to fight exhibition bouts for the Nazis, who later murdered him.

Abe "Newsboy" Hollandersky, while in the navy distributing newspapers to sailors, famously sparred with Teddy Roosevelt and fought more professional bouts than anyone in history. Wallach the Fighting Dentist supposedly fixed the teeth of K. O. Brown that he had punched out the night before. Many went on to staid Jewish careers.

But the most loved was "Pride of the Ghetto" Beryl David Rosofsky—Barney Ross—a 127-pound fighter who would hold world championships in three weight classes. Raised Orthodox, he sometimes spoke Yiddish and studied Talmud while training. He entered the ring with the Star of David on his robe and trunks, to the strains of "My Yiddishe Momma," which always drew Jewish tears.

As Hitler rose and anti-Semitism surged in America, Jews—even ultra-Orthodox yeshiva students—huddled around their radios for blow by blows of Ross's fights. Often the names of his opponents—Al Santora, Tony Canzoneri, Jimmy McLarnin—meant intense ethnic rivalry. Shouts of "Kill the dirty little Jew!" were heard at Madison Square Garden. The pinnacle was his three-fight world-championship series with McLarnin, who was called the "Jewish Nemesis" and the "Scourge of the Fighting Sons of Israel." He easily beat many Jewish boxers, even the great Benny Leonard, who had come out of retirement to defend Jewish honor.

Eleven days before the series, the same Garden held twenty thousand swastika-bearing American Nazis, so a lot was at stake. Ross won the first fight and had a ticker-tape parade. He said, "The Irish are the greatest of sportsmen. I'm almost ashamed I beat one." He briefly delayed the rematch for the Jewish High Holidays and lost that by a split decision but won the third hands down. He and McLarnin became lifelong friends, exchanging cards at their respective religious holidays.

Ross was finally beaten by "the Human Buzzsaw," the outstanding African American fighter Henry Armstrong; Ross took so much pummeling that fans screamed to stop the fight. He went the distance but retired; he was too old—going on twenty-nine. But four years later, with an age waiver, he enlisted as a private in the Marines. Severely wounded at Guadalcanal, he won the Silver Star, a Sergeant's stripes, and his fans' adulation.

But he now had to battle the drugs prescribed for his wounds. His voluntary treatment tapered the morphine over ten days, but he went cold turkey on day five. The next five, he said, worsted his thirteen hours almost bleeding to death in a Guadalcanal ditch and made Armstrong's hammering seem easy. He returned to give staunch moral and public support (he could not get permission to fight) for Israel's War for Independence.

Jewish boxing has been in eclipse for decades, although there are signs of a comeback among—not surprisingly—recent immigrants from Israel. There have been other great Jewish sports heroes: Hank Greenberg and Sandy Koufax in baseball, Mark Spitz in swimming, and the tragic heroes of the 1972 Israeli Olympic team who died at the peak of their strength and form, in Munich no less, murdered en masse by Palestinian terrorists. But it is no small irony that the people known for their lack of physical stamina and reluctance to fight made their greatest athletic reputation in the "sweet science" of punching other bodies.

Meanwhile, other Jews fought in the street.[2] Some ran prostitution rings and participated fully in the international white slave trade. Many Jews were prostitutes themselves, some "willingly," taking their best chance to escape poverty. Motche Goldberg and other pimps built thriving brothel-chains, and by 1910, one Jewish reporter could write, "The traffic of Jewesses is almost worldwide."[3] In Buenos Aires, half the prostitutes and half the madams were Jews. Gambling in New York City's Lower East Side was at first run by Irish mobsters like Big Tim Sullivan, but he hired "smart young Jewboys" like Herman Rosenthal and Arnold Rothstein, who was raised Orthodox but whose father sat shivah for him when he took a Gentile bride.

Networks of thieves, pickpockets, fences, pimps, enforcers, and arsonists staked out the Lower East Side, a lot of them Jews. Monk Eastman's bullet-shaped head, wild hair, and ferocious look matched the brass knuckles, blackjacks, and pistols he used to thrash his enemies (women, though, he hit only with his bare hands). His protection gang kept street thugs (including themselves) away from brothels and

"Big Jack" Zelig (Zelig Lefkowitz), around 1912.
Jack charged $10 for a slash to the cheek, progressing
up to $100 for murder.
Used by permission of Bettmann/CORBIS.

gambling emporiums and shielded scabs from union workers
on strike. Max "Kid Twist" Zwerbach took over when Monk
went to Sing Sing.

"Big Jack" Zelig, together with Lefty Louie Rosenberg,
and Harry Horowitz ("Gyp the Blood"), who could break
your back with his bare hands, were rent-a-thugs: $10 for a
knife slash to the cheek, $25 for a bullet in the arm or leg, $50
for bomb-throwing, and $100 for murder. They killed John
"Spanish Louie" Lewis, a Sephardic Jew who wore black
clothes and a sombrero. Later an Italian rival, Jules Morello,

strode into a casino yelling, "Where's that big Yid Zelig? I gotta cook that big Yid!" but Big Jack cooked him first.

Fresh out of Sing Sing, Dopey Benny Fein took a balanced approach to industrial relations, hiring his men out as both company goons and union thugs. He handled the garment trade, while furriers and bakers belonged to Joe "the Greaser" Rosenzweig and his disciples. Yoski "Nigger" Toblinsky's gang (the Jewish Black Hand Association, expert at stealing and poisoning horses) got the Teamsters, Johnny Levinsky got the ice-cream franchise, Charley "the Cripple" Vitoffsky the soda and seltzer deliveries.[4]

But World War I drew large numbers of Jewish volunteers. Those who came back moved up, had smaller families, and left the city. Jewish mobs dried up, but the dry years of Prohibition brought them back. Waxey Gordon was an out-of-work *schlammer*—Yiddish for limb-breaker—when he met Big Maxey Greenberg.[5] With Arnold Rothstein they imported Scotch, hired goons to protect it, and became bootleg millionaires.

But Jews didn't drink a lot, so to keep their Gentile market share the Jewish gangs became especially violent. Dutch Schultz (Arthur Flegenheimer) terrorized the South Bronx. "Little Jerusalem" was a Detroit neighborhood run by Sammy "Purple" Cohen and the Fleisher and Bernstein brothers. Minneapolis belonged to Yiddy and Harry Bloom and Kid Cann, Kansas City to Solomon "Cutcher-Head-Off" Weissman, Newark to Longy Zwillman, Philly to Nig Rosen and Boo Boo Hoff, and Boston to Hyman Abrams and

"King" Solomon. Al Capone and Bugs Moran ran Chicago, but a few Jews got their share.

Improbable friendships arose. Lucky Luciano, who as a boy ate Friday night dinners with Jewish friends, teamed with Meyer Lansky, Bugsy Siegel, and Dutch Schultz. Frank Costello, who married his Jewish childhood sweetheart, brought some Jews to a mob conclave and Vito Genovese yelled, "What are you trying to do, load us down with a bunch of Hebes?" Costello said calmly, "Take it easy, Don Vitone, you're nothin' but a fuckin' foreigner yourself."

Louis Buchalter—"Czar Lepke"—built Murder, Inc., in the twenties, and growing up in Brooklyn I knew a man who had run errands for them as a boy. They "protected" the garment industry, and later, along with Italian and other mobs, the Hollywood movie studios. Lepke's Wanted poster offered $25,000 "dead or alive," describing him as 5- foot- 5½, white, and Jewish. "Eyes, piercing and shifting; nose, large, somewhat blunt at nostrils; ears, prominent and close to head . . . Frequents baseball games." Schultz and his gang were wiped out one night in a Newark chop house by Charlie "the Bug" Workman and Mendy Weiss. Dutch was cut down at the urinal. Lepke got the electric chair in 1944.

Growing up in then-very-Jewish Brooklyn, I was not taught to admire these men. But for boys who were sometimes beaten up or robbed of our few coins when we walked past Our Lady Help of Christians church, it was nice to know that somewhere there were Jews that tough. Some of them, including Zwillman, Lansky, and Mickey Cohen, broke up Nazi meetings in the U.S. and beat up the brown shirts and went on to run guns to the Jews in Israel after the massive Arab invasion in the late forties.[7] So they were also defending *us*.

Back in 1910 on the Lower East Side an Italian gang was bullying Jews; Big Jack Zelig's gang dressed up like Orthodox men, surprised the Italians, beat them senseless, and ran them out of the neighborhood. Such collective memories last a long time. Just as countless Jews crowded their radios for Ross's fights, some of us also felt a guilty, secret thrill in the vicious, raw, physical power of these fearless Jewish outlaws. After the Holocaust, there was another fantasy image: Adolf Hitler alone for fifteen minutes with any one of them.

12

The Trowel and the Sword

In Israel today, the relationship between body and book can be complex. For instance, when television news covers suicide bombings of civilians in Israel, you often see bearded men in skullcaps with sidelocks going up and down the street or through the destroyed bus or restaurant retrieving pieces of all the bodies. In Orthodox belief, a person's body must be buried with all its parts—a challenge with bombs, rockets, artillery shells, or hand grenades. Others tend to the wounded, but they follow the Torah's imperative to bury the dead "on the same day," and nothing must be left unburied. They call this *chesed shel emes*—true kindness—an unconditional gift to those who cannot even give thanks, and they say that this work makes God smile. They have been honored in Israel even by many who resent the grip of Orthodoxy because they have the courage to run toward what everyone else is running away from.

A high school friend of mine is an ultra-Orthodox rabbi in Israel—and also a professor of classics. My visits with him help me get inside the minds of Israelis who view the world from within the Torah. He has done *chesed shel emes*, even for an enemy soldier, in the 1982 war, some years after moving to Israel. He has explained to me with great patience why ultra-Orthodox boys cannot serve in the army, when almost every other Israeli boy has to, including modern-Orthodox boys who serve and study in alternation and are among the country's bravest fighters; but the most religious say it would deal a crippling blow to the next generation of scholars, and Orthodox girls would therefore not be able to find suitable husbands. Still, fear has little to do with it; picking up body parts at the front right after a battle or under fire is not the act of those afraid of war.

In fact, the Orthodox view of these deaths, whether at the front in a war or in a Jerusalem pizzeria in peacetime, is that they are "sanctifications of G–d's name." This is more sacralized, but otherwise not so different, from the view taken by most Israelis and most Jews. Since the day God promised the land to Abraham—or if you are secular, since the time thousands of years ago when the Jewish people arose in the land—Jews have had to fight to hold on to every inch of it that was theirs (and perhaps some that were not). To die for the Holy Land is both heroic and sacred, and each year on Remembrance Day when those deaths are marked, Israelis do not hold barbecues, picnics, and races. They stop at noon for a full minute, whatever they are doing—driving, teaching, cooking, farming—and stand in silent remembrance.

The Six-Day War of 1967 was a watershed for Israel, but also for Jews in the United States, where non-Jews began to see them in a different way, and some were remarkably frank about their surprise. A man pumping gas in South Georgia

The cover of a Syrian army reading-and-writing primer
from the 1960s, *Salem in the Army*, shows caricatured Jews
drowning in the Mediterranean while a Syrian
infantryman trods on the flag of Israel.

said, "Them's damn fightin' Jews. I always thought Jews
were yaller, but those Jews, man, they're tough."[1] A
businessman said to one of his Jewish associates, "You Hebes
really taught those guys a lesson." In fact, American Jews
had mostly just watched, but they soon understood that the
army of Israel had struck a blow for their own reputation,

too, and that the notion of Jewish physical softness and fear of fighting would never again be quite so plausible to so many; it was a turning point in the history of the Jewish body.

I remember my first visit to Mount Herzl, where the military graves are: so many young people. Our tour guide—we were a group of Jewish college professors who had never been to the country before—was looking particularly sad, so I asked her as gently as possible, "Do you have someone here?" She was a very polite and helpful person, so I am sure that the look of contempt she cast my way was completely involuntary. "*Are you a fool?*" her eyes seemed to ask, "*Everyone has someone here.*" A country of warriors is also a country of mourners.

On that trip I got a glimpse of a world of courage and grief that I would marvel at on seven subsequent trips to Israel and during much of the time in between. Talk about the people of the body. *True Grit* was the name of one of John Wayne's movies, but the man couldn't hold the hem of the average Israeli's trousers. Not that this was news to me. I had both known and felt it since I had learned to talk, in the time of the Nuremberg Trials and Israel's War of Independence. I am not quite two years older than the state, and the simultaneous realization of the almost unbelievable weakness and vulnerability of the Jews with their heroic physical force and strength were formative for me.

My boyhood fantasy life included a lot of musing about my namesake and what he would have done to the Germans had he and his B-25 made it to Europe. Our front stoop was

Cannon muzzles of eight Arab states: Sudan, Algeria,
United Arab Republic (now Egypt and Syria), Saudi
Arabia, Jordan, Iraq, Syria, and Lebanon. Lebanese daily
Al-Jarida, May 31, 1967.

an ideal shape for a bomber crew, although my friends were
sometimes puzzled when I insisted on being the copilot. The
rabbi in my Orthodox synagogue certainly preached about
the revival of the Jewish state and our responsibility toward
it. I was thirteen when the paperback of *Exodus* came out—
we couldn't afford hardcover books or, certainly, a trip to
Israel—and I read it avidly, enraptured by the story of the
country's painful founding, enamored of (yes, Gentile) Kitty
Fremont, dreaming day and night of becoming as strong and
brave as Ari Ben Canaan.

But that was fantasy; Israel was real. Although I knew
about the successes of the Israel Defense Forces, it was still
somehow surprising to see boys and girls with Jewish faces,
in uniform, with Uzis slung over their shoulders. I can still

"The barricades in Tel-Aviv," appearing in the Syrian
Army organ *Al-Jundi Al-Arabi*, June 6, 1967.

remember the handsome young men in naval uniforms we
saw when we went to the illegal-immigration museum in
Haifa; I somehow had not considered that Israel must also
have a navy. And while climbing up Masada—the site of a
mass Jewish suicide to prevent a surrender to the Romans—
I looked up toward an unsettling roar to see the Star of
David emblazoned on the wings of a pair of fighter jets, light
glinting off them in a brief, dazzling dance; the relief was
palpable.

I got to know real heroes. My friend Pazit, for instance,
was a casualty officer with an armored force on the Golan
Heights in the 1973 war. Her husband, Michael, who piloted
a helicopter in the Sinai during the same war, was a sitting
duck for snipers and rocket fire. A professor I know at the

Hebrew University told me about entering Jerusalem in 1967 with his unit, Jews going freely to the Western Wall for the first time since the Temple was destroyed. A middle-aged *kibbutznik* I met had single-handedly fought and killed a pair of terrorists who had infiltrated the community. A friend who is a retired lieutenant colonel in the reserves, who immigrated from England not long after the war for independence, had been in too many wars to mention, and he didn't want them mentioned anyway. The list goes on.

And then there was the next generation. Pazit and Mikhail's vibrant, self-confident oldest daughter served in a high-priority intelligence unit so secret that she could not tell her parents what she was doing. (The old Israeli joke says, "so secret even I don't know what I'm doing," which can also be true.) Her brilliant, sensitive younger sister, studying comparative literature in college, gave me lessons one night in Jerusalem as we strolled after dinner, pointing out—reluctantly, as with most Israelis, because I dragged it out of her—the features of various automatic rifles on shoulders that we passed along the way; before becoming a student of humanities, then law, she too was in military intelligence. And the youngest, their heartthrob of a brother, came home one weekend while I was visiting. He was a senior in high school, just back from a grueling weekend of physical competition to become eligible for an elite army unit: weight-lifting, endurance, races with forty-pound packs on your back—the stuff of Max Nordau's dreams. He placed in the top four out of hundreds, and his unstoppable grin looked like it had to be hurting his face.

Afterwards I talked with his father—now a high-tech company manager and a yoga master, he exuded a quiet, retiring but confident masculinity—about whether this wouldn't land his son in the most dangerous situations. No, he said, the elite units do dangerous things, but you are surrounded by the very best people. He was proud of his son, of course, but dismayed that this gifted and beautiful boy would have to learn, like his parents and grandparents before him, to fight for his own country's life. He became an airborne navigator. One day at a bus stop I saw two boys in air force officers' uniforms. Are you flying today? I asked them. One looked up with a calm, pale, gentle, handsome face and said matter-of-factly, "We fly every day." I did not have to think I would approve of every command they might follow in order to feel strengthened and comforted.

These are a few brave people among millions. I would like to think that I could have been like them, but I will never know. I actively opposed the war in Vietnam, and I have never served in uniform in combat or otherwise. I have done some mildly dangerous things, as anthropologists will, and certainly some uncomfortable and physically demanding ones. But how would I have acquitted myself if I had had to fight for something I believed in? Most of us want to think we would be heroes, but heroes are special people and there are not very many of them.

I don't by any means discount the suffering of the Palestinian people, some of whom I know and admire. They are, to be sure, also victims of history, and the much greater suffering of the Jews is central to that history. But they are also

From a Bahrain newspaper, June 2002. The Jew: "Say 'I hate the Arabs.' " The parrot Bush repeats it twice. Bahrain was designated a "Major Non-NATO Ally" of the United States in October 2001.

From a collection of anti-Semitic cartoons compiled from the Arab media by journalist and media analyst Tom Gross (www.tomgrossmedia.com).

victims of the relentless hostility of the larger Arab world to the Jews' return to their ancient homeland; of that larger world's cynical encouragement of Palestinian recalcitrance and terrorist violence; and of the violent expulsion of Jews from almost all the Arab lands where they had lived for many centuries—an expulsion larger than the one that affected the Palestinians in Israel after the state was born. Nevertheless, like most Israeli Jews, I favor the establishment of an independent Palestinian state within the next few years.

Still, it is interesting how the themes and imagery of classic European and Nazi anti-Semitism have now been adopted by Israel's Arab enemies. Within the past few years, a long dramatic series based on *The Protocols of the Elders of Zion*, a fantasy tract about how a small cabal of Jews runs the world, had great success on Arab television. Cartoons in leading newspapers, schoolbooks, and army primers depict Jews as the Nazis did. Ironically, most Jews in Israel are descendants of refugees from Arab lands; they look like their Arab neighbors, not the European Jews in the caricatures.

Nor are they cartoon farmer-warriors. As my friend Pazit wrote, "the change of attitude toward the body [also includes] sports and fitness, extreme physical adventures, awareness of preventive health care, ballet, drama and martial arts, and fashion and hedonistic/leisure activities, which were not part of my grandparents' life." Yet most of those athletes, dancers, and fashionistas have been soldiers. At times I feel an undeserved, vicarious, almost mystical strength coming from across the sea. I am an unrepentant, dyed-in-the-wool American, but also a Jew, and I am glad to know that such Jews exist. Max Nordau wrote, "Let us once more become deep-chested, sturdy, sharp-eyed men"; he thought it would take centuries. Emma Lazarus asked, "Where are the warrior-mechanics of today?" *Well, they have come. Now, by the million, they are here and they are real.*

13

The Eye of the Beholder

Nordau's interest in healing the Jewish body, although tragically comforting to anti-Semites of his time and even to the Nazi doctors to come, reflected a centuries-long Jewish devotion to medicine. Jews made up about 60 percent of the physicians in Berlin in the mid-1930s, when Gentile patients were forbidden to go to them—a windfall for their Aryan colleagues. This remarkably successful Jewish focus took the skills of scholarship and inquiry honed through Torah and Talmud study and applied them not to ideas but to the body itself—the life of the mind examining the body. In a sense it was an extension of the concerns of Talmudic Rabbis. But prominent Jewish physicians, often also community leaders, shaped the ideas about health and illness held by other Jews.

One of the ironies is that in the late nineteenth century, as Jewish physicians became ever more numerous, they, like their Gentile counterparts, were convinced that Jews were racially distinct—an idea that strengthened its hold in every decade—with critical consequences for health. Jewish doctors owed it to their Jewish patients to take the best care of them, and given the fin de siècle understanding of race and medicine, this meant viewing them through a seriously distorting but widely accepted racial lens. So as Sander Gilman has shown in *The Jew's Body*, Jewish physicians were both subject and object. To be good doctors in that era, they had to take "the other's" perspective on their own irreparable "otherness," but the racial lens they borrowed often gave them a dim and twisted view of their people, their patients, and themselves.

The Apollonian ideal of Greece and Rome had been the ideal of the European upper classes for twenty centuries, and the "Aryan" racial ideal was a biologized version of that, the pinnacle of health, strength, and beauty. And while a religious and cultural choice—circumcision—formed a barrier to Jewish Apollonian aspirations in the ancient Greco-Roman world, the modern barrier was blood or, technically, genes. In the late-nineteenth-century account, accepted by physicians Jewish and non-Jewish alike, the flaws of the Jewish body were intrinsic, not acquired, and it formed a perfect foil to the Aryan/Apollonian model.

Jews were supposedly subject to nervous-system weakness, diabetes, tuberculosis, flat feet, and many other ailments—perhaps most insidiously, syphilis—at rates that, through this lens, looked much higher than for other Europeans. They had distinctive and unhealthy skin, hair, feet, voices, body odor (the *foetor Judaicus*, supposedly due to male menstruation), and, most prominently, noses. By the

Nazi era, we have seen, these stereotypes were reinforced, deepened, codified, expanded, and yet so finely drawn that even a Jew who could "pass" could supposedly be detected by a well-trained German child. A few decades earlier, the consequences were subtler but still thoroughly pernicious. Although the great German physician and public health pioneer Rudolf Virchow had studied ten thousand children and reported in 1886 that Jews were physically indistinguishable from non-Jews, this fact was lost in a cultural climate of racial theory.

Strange to say, one of the more damaging stereotypes was that Jews had flat feet.[1] This was far more important than it sounds and integral to the exclusion and stigmatization of Jews, because it excluded them from army service and so was strongly tied to the stereotype of Jews as unable to fight. A dubious study of Austrian Jews in 1804 stated that because of "weak feet," most Jews inducted into the military were released early and that this was because "the majority of Jewish soldiers spent more time in the military hospitals than in military service." This report was one salvo in a century-long debate about Jews' fitness to serve.

Infantry are not called foot soldiers for nothing—as one of my uncles said of his World War I combat, "A soldier's job is not to think; a soldier's job is to slog with your feet through the mud and get killed." If flat feet impeded marching and Jews had flat feet, ergo, Jews were unfit to serve. Nothing less than Jewish emancipation was at stake; a people who could not fight for their country could not be full and equal citizens.

The author in 1979 at the U.S. Military Cemetery at Meuse-Argonne,
where many Americans who fell in World War I are buried.
Photo by Marjorie Shostak. Used by permission of the Estate of Marjorie Shostak.

The stereotype persisted despite many counterexamples.
Theodor Fontane, a commentator on the war of 1866, wrote
that three Jewish reservists had been mobilized as part of
the first battalion of the prince's own regiment. "One, no
longer young and corpulent, suffered horribly. His feet were
open sores. He fought in the burning sun from the beginning
to the end of the battle. . . . He could not be persuaded to go
into hospital before the battle."[2] Yet even this defense of
Jewish honor exemplifies the Jewish soldier as being corpulent and having weak feet; Jews are not normal, but *despite*
their racial weaknesses, the defender claims, they can fight.

Most Jews who became officers converted along the way.

Fontane considered their ambition for military careers as evidence of a desired transformation: "It seemed as if the Jews had promised themselves to make an end of their old notions about their dislike for war and inability to engage in it." Jews served in not only the Austrian and German armies, but in those of almost all European nations throughout the nineteenth century, often fighting against one another. There was said to have been a Dutch Jewish artilleryman at Waterloo who yelled *Shema Yisrael!* above the explosion each time he fired a shell. A fellow soldier explained, "It may be some Yehudee gets killed by him, and he could never pardon himself, if any one of his brethren should, through him, go out of the world without *Shemos*"— without the *Shema*.

Jewish physicians and medical scientists became actively engaged in the debate over Jewish weakness in general and flat-footedness in particular. They accepted the characterization but argued that these features were not hereditary and immutable. Rather, they resulted from the social conditions of a people weakened by poverty and exclusion and at the same time had neglected their bodies in favor of their minds, for many centuries. Max Nordau, the founder of "Muscle-Jewry," had written of how the ghetto deprived Jews of all the Aristotelian elements—earth, air, light, and water; how Jewish limbs forgot their gay movements; how Jewish eyes began to blink shyly in sunless houses; how Jewish voices became frightened whispers.[3]

"Nordau's cry," Gilman writes, was "that we have killed

our bodies in the stinking streets of the ghettoes and we must now rebuild them on the playing fields of Berlin and Vienna."[4] One might add, under the gaze of Apollo.

Although there was debate about the question, the predominant view from the 1600s was that Jews were black—or at least not white. Houston Stewart Chamberlain, the historian who shaped Nazi racial theory, held that Jews were a mongrel race that had mixed with Africans in ancient Alexandria. According to another theorist, Robert Knox, Jews had an "African character," including a "muzzle-shaped mouth and face" as well as "lips very full, mouth projecting, chin small," and indeed "the whole physiognomy, when swarthy, as it often is, has an African look."[5] The darkness of the Jew's skin was also thought to be associated with syphilis and a sign of predisposition to hysteria.

As early as 1862, the German-*Jewish* revolutionary Moses Hess wrote—without apparent irony—that "even baptism will not redeem the German Jew from the nightmare of German Jew-hatred. The Germans hate less the religion of the Jews than their race. . . . Jewish noses cannot be reformed, nor black, curly, Jewish hair be turned through baptism or combing into smooth hair. . . . The Jewish type is indestructible."[6] Thus it was clear to some that the growing number of voluntary Jewish conversions to Christianity to gain acceptance and move ahead in life (as Heinrich Heine, and the families of Felix Mendelssohn, Karl Marx, Benjamin Disraeli, and many others had done), or for that matter the early Reform movement in Judaism with its effort to mimic liberal Protestantism and remove the stigma of Orthodox practices, would be of no avail, since Jewish separateness (and Jewish defects) were racial.

But it didn't stop some Jews from trying. Hair was straightened and dyed blond, eyebrows trimmed and plucked, skin bleached, and ears tucked back closer to the skull in innovative surgical procedures. And, in the greatest step in the cosmetic surgery of the era, Jewish noses were straightened and "bobbed"—cut short—to remove this most obvious and "indestructible" Jewish stigma. But as Gilman has thoroughly shown, in the mind of Christian Europe the Jew's nose was not just a cosmetic deformity. It was a prelude to and consequence of disease, a sign of financial shrewdness, and a marker of defective sexuality. None other than Sigmund Freud and his surgeon friend Wilhelm Fliess famously treated a number of patients (mostly women), with Fliess operating on their noses to "cure" their psychiatric ailments—even then a highly dubious strategy.

But there was another pioneering operation on the Jewish nose, one that has come down to us today, and not just for Jews. It is the rhinoplasty, developed by Jewish surgeon Jacques (né Jakob) Joseph. Born in 1865, Joseph straddled Jewish and Gentile worlds, with a main allegiance to the latter. Like many men of the period, including more than a few Jews, he proudly bore the lifelong facial scars he acquired as a young fraternity duelist. He had been what young Germans in those days liked to call *Satisfaktionsfähig*—worthy of satisfaction—a great compliment for a Jew. Those facial dueling scars, often manipulated during healing to make them more prominent—much as many African cultures do in their scarification rites—were displayed by men of a certain social standing to show all who gazed on them that they had had the courage to satisfy or be satisfied in a duel and that other young men of similar background and character had admitted them to this privileged fraternity.

Attempts were made to block upwardly mobile Jews from acquiring these lifelong marks of courage and acceptance. In 1896 (Hitler was seven in that year), a group of dueling fraternities decreed that since

> there exists between Aryans and Jews such a deep moral and psychic difference, and that our qualities have suffered so much through Jewish mischief, in full consideration of the many proofs which the Jewish student has also given of his lack of honor and character and since he is completely void of honor according to our German concepts, today's conference . . . resolves: "No satisfaction is to be given to a Jew with any weapon, as he is unworthy of it."[7]

This symbolic slap in the face was a far more grievous insult than the actual slap with a glove that led to many duels and it hurt more than those sought-after rapier gashes. But Jakob Joseph had slipped in before the ban, and for the rest of his life he could hold his head high and show the scars of the code of honor.

No doubt this bit of "accidental" cosmetic surgery, which

he had avidly sought to make himself more German, helped him to understand that transformations of the face can challenge racial destiny. As a leading orthopedic surgeon he had mended countless broken limbs but also corrected congenital conditions like clubfeet to make the lives of people born with imperfect bodies better. But the head of his surgical group dismissed him when Joseph fixed a child's protruding ears. Surgery to correct clubfeet was reconstructive and functional; surgery to pin back ears was vanity, and there was, it seemed, a world of ethical and professional difference between the two.

After his own ears were thus symbolically pinned back, Joseph opened a private practice and was soon approached by a young man deeply troubled by his protruding nose. Joseph corrected his "condition" in the first modern rhinoplasty. Reporting to the Berlin Medical Society in 1898, he emphasized that "the psychological effect of the operation is of utmost importance. The depressed attitude . . . subsided completely. He is happy to move around unnoticed . . . the patient who formerly avoided social contact now wishes to attend and give parties."[8] Like the procedure Freud got involved in, this was a nose operation that cured psychological problems, but not through any elaborate theory. It was common sense with a dollop of sociology: If you can't measure up to the prevailing standard of beauty, and if this is a racial stigma that makes you unhappy and holds you back, why not have a doctor change the way you look?

In a land where hundreds of thousands of purely cosmetic surgeries are done every year, and in which nearly every face or body over forty we see on the mass media has had something done to it, most of us accept this as legitimate. A hundred years ago surgery was riskier and social opprobrium common; nevertheless, cosmetic procedures were devised and Jews used them early and often. Joseph himself bobbed many Jewish noses. As Gilman puts it, he made his patients less visible in their world.

Sixteen-year-old Adolphine Schwarz had her nose fixed by Joseph, as her brother had done before her. They were a family of small means and she later recalled, "When he felt that someone suffered from a 'Jewish nose,' he would operate for free."[9] As one plastic surgeon put it, "The line between reconstructive rhinoplasty and cosmetic rhinoplasty is a fine one. Just how unusual a nose must look to cause distress is relative."[10] Although two American physicians had developed similar techniques at around the same time, to a German surgeon America was a medical backwater. Joseph was an independent pioneer, and his students included some who came from the United States to learn the techniques of the master.

Yet the specialty already had a substantial history. Medical and "scientific" references to the Jewish nose go back at least to 1850, when Robert Knox (also known for pseudo-scientific writings on the inferiority of Africans) described it as "a large, massive, club-shaped, hooked nose, three or four times larger than suits the face. . . . Thus it is that the Jewish face never can [be], and never is, perfectly beautiful."[11] But after Jacques Joseph made this fixable, it was no longer a matter of abstract "scientific" interest, and by the

1920s, medical writings on rhinoplasty often referred explicitly to the Jewish nose.

In the journal *Laryngoscope* in 1930, one surgeon wrote that "the modification of accentuated family or racial characteristics, such as are sometimes observable especially in Semitic subjects . . . is frequently of great importance to the individual." Another wrote in the *Journal of the American Dental Association* in 1936, in the context of growing anti-Semitic prejudice, that "change in the shape of the pronounced Jewish nose may be sought for either social or business reasons." These and many other articles of the period on cosmetic (aesthetic) surgery were in part attempts to establish legitimacy by showing that more was at stake than vanity; disabled people were being helped.

Others saw it differently. When Fanny Brice (Fania Borach), the famous Jewish comedian played by Barbra Streisand in the movie *Funny Girl*, had her nose done in 1923, the brilliant satirist Dorothy Parker wrote the WASPy (and waspish) comment that Brice "cut off her nose to spite her race."[12] Brice never hid her Jewishness before or after, but clearly she had wanted a different face. (Parker herself was born a New Jersey Rothschild but with her Scottish mother's nose.)

In 1945, Bess Myerson, who had been Miss New York City, became the first Jewish Miss America. Despite pressure to change her name, she took pride in her Jewish identity and overcame considerable prejudice both before and after winning the pageant. She went on to a varied and successful

Andy Warhol's *Before and After*, 1962.
Used by permission of the Artists Rights Society, agent for the Andy Warhol Foundation for Visual Arts. © 2008 *Andy Warhol Foundation for the Visual Arts / ARS, New York.*

career, partly in New York City government, supported charitable causes including Jewish ones, and never traded obviously on her looks. But Bess Myerson did not look particularly Jewish.

By the 1960s, "nose jobs" were commonplace, and especially popular among teenage Jewish girls. High school students of that era in New York and other cities with large Jewish populations will remember as I do how common it was to see a girl come back from spring break with a small bandage over the bridge of her nose and later to learn to look at her differently. It has been aptly called a kind of circumcision into the Gentile world, and with the opposite effect: as a boy was deliberately separated from that world by his circumcision, a girl could be blended into it by hers.

As one writer put it, "you could say that Jews were some of the early trend setters" in plastic surgery. "Jews, who have always had a love/hate relationship with plastic surgery—and their own appearance—have helped create a trend that has now exploded into the mainstream. . . . Jews, out of their very desire to appear less Jewish, made plastic surgery acceptable to the very people whom they were trying to look like."[13] Dissatisfaction, once racial, became increasingly universal.

There are no good statistics, but these operations appear to have peaked in the sixties and seventies. This was the early baby boom in the wake of the Nazi era. According to James Baker, a plastic surgeon with a practice near Orlando, "Jewish parents at that time didn't want their children to look Jewish. They feared a stigma left from the war." Dr. Thomas Rees, who trained many Park Avenue plastic surgeons, put it more bluntly: "Everybody wanted to look like a shiksa."[14]

A woman I once took an interest in told me that her exquisite face was partly man-made. Spiritually and ethnically she was Jewish to her core, but she had had a rhinoplasty years earlier and still felt like an impostor. What was once a cure for alienation and inequality now caused anxiety and guilt; she felt she did not deserve the attention she got from men. She was no less beautiful for having told me this and our flirtation was star-crossed for weightier reasons, but it did enter my mind that if she and I were to have a daughter, there would be a loud cultural echo of her mother's own experience along about the ninth or tenth grade. What would we have done?

It is now no longer clear. Statistics do not cover the whole period from the seventies until now, but it seems that rhinoplasty among Jews has gone into decline. For a time during the nineties, while total cosmetic surgeries more than doubled, nose jobs declined. Could it have been the influence of Barbra Streisand? A more inclusive notion of beauty that now includes many ethnic standards, not just that of northern Europe? A greater pride in being Jewish? Or just a greater distance from what Europe did to the Jews?

We don't know. These surgeries have increased again in the past few years, but there is no information about how many Jews have sought them. Tori Spelling, Roseanne Barr, Kate Hudson, Gwyneth Paltrow (of the Paltrowitz line), Natalie Portman (née Hershlag), and Winona Ryder (née Horowitz) are among the recent celebrities of Jewish descent said to have had plastic surgery on their noses; Streisand certainly did not put an end to them. (Clearly it is not always easy to answer the question, "Did she or didn't she?" but there is a lively interest on the Internet in comparing certain women's earlier and later photos.)

The idea that specifically *Jewish* noses often need correcting remains current among cosmetic surgeons. Two recent textbooks refer specifically to the Jewishness of certain noses.[15] The 1996 textbook *Aesthetic Rhinoplasty* by F. V. Nicolle states that correcting the "Jewish nose" should be done "with lowering of the dorsum, narrowing of the bony pyramid, refinement and elevation of the excessively long hanging tip." A 1998 textbook of facial aesthetic surgery describes two patients whose noses "have acute nasolabial angles, plunging tips, or foreshortened nasal tip pyramids" and states that they were of "Jewish ancestry" or descent.

One Jewish author puts it bluntly. Virginia L. Blum, in *Flesh Wounds: The Culture of Cosmetic Surgery*, writes, "Certain kinds of noses speak Jewishness. . . . Jews assimilating into a largely gentile culture thus strip from our features the traces of our ethnicity. . . . We straighten curly hair, dye dark hair light. We get very thin to disguise what we often imagine are Jewish-coded thighs and hips. What we choose to treat are precisely the features that are culturally selected as our distinguishing physical traits." Her use of the word *treat* rather than *change* reflects the general acceptance of medicalized racial identity.

Since Jews are not really white, if we want acceptance we, like some African Americans, straighten and bleach our hair, try to keep our skin from darkening, slim our thighs and buttocks, and surgically change our faces so that we look more like the social and cultural elite. Minorities always have their bodies and faces judged by a standard designed for someone else. Jews are perhaps born closer than some to the cultural ideal, but at times that has made things worse for them, when a backlash of revulsion tried to make the distinctions hard-and-fast.

Some interesting observations come from an Orthodox Jewish plastic surgeon. "When you look at studies of what people feel is attractive, it's symmetry. Things that are out of proportion are viewed as unattractive. This is across cultural lines. . . . I come from a family where four out of five kids wanted rhinoplasty. I don't think they wanted to look Swedish. I think they all had beaks."[16]

Excuse me? They had *beaks*? In fairness to the doctor, he means that it was not any desire to escape their ethnicity but rather having a kind of deformity that motivated them to seek surgery. Their noses were "out of proportion" and therefore "viewed as unattractive . . . across cultural lines." Is it possible that there is a universal, even absolute standard of beauty that has nothing to do with cultural preferences? Artists at least since the Renaissance have toyed with ideas about such absolutes, some even using geometric and mathematical approaches to discover the ideally proportioned face and body.

More recently psychologists and evolutionary biologists have conducted studies that suggest a few conclusions. First, different people rank bodies and faces similarly, in almost any combination of the race and culture of either the raters or the rated. Second, high-ranking (beautiful) people get more positive attention when they are babies, schoolchildren, job applicants, running for election, on the witness stand, seeking mates (of course), and even when they are dead on arrival in an emergency room. In our politically correct era, beauty is the last bastion of accepted unfair advantage, and the most neglected; it gives the lucky member of the club an edge in every stage and walk of life. Third, not only beauty itself but the perception of beauty appears to have biological foundations.

There are of course exceptions. Piercings, markings, and adornment are cultural. Preferred weight varies a lot (most cultures have had a plump, not a thin, ideal), although waist-to-hip ratio does not. Gender-specific preferences in facial proportions (judgments of masculinity and femininity) show some interesting cultural twists. But there is no way to look objectively at the facts and conclude either that beauty is unimportant or that it is all culturally determined.

What explains the patterns we consistently find beautiful? A waist-to-hip ratio of about three-fourths allows the casual male viewer to conclude that a woman is probably not pregnant; men who ignored this signal might have been disadvantaged in evolutionary competition. The reason that most cultures prefer plump women—as in ancient statues of Aphrodite and Renaissance paintings—is that a little plumpness ensures that a woman can sustain a pregnancy and a period of lactation if a man has the luck to mate with her. The most attractive male bodies have broad shoulders and narrow waists and hips, enabling an ideal blend of strength and agility; this shape, not surprisingly, is Apollo's.

Please understand: This is not how I think things should be, but how I think they are. With faces the issues are different, but the research allows us to cut through the confusion with four main principles:

First, gender matters: masculinity—a large jaw, prominent brows, and a five o'clock shadow, all features related to testosterone level—is usually attractive to women, although some prefer more androgynous men; the opposite features are most attractive to men. Second, because women's reproductive capacity is more age-limited than is the case for men, men have evolved a bias toward youthful-looking women. (Men also age out of both reproductive capacity and attractiveness, but later.) During our evolution, women on average had their first menstruation around age sixteen and their first child around three years later. Men who were strongly attracted to women this age would have had greater reproductive success. Third, symmetry matters—not the symmetry that the Orthodox surgeon was talking about but simple bilateral symmetry: Is the right side of the face the mirror image of the left? All faces are asymmetrical to some extent, but asymmetry that goes beyond this normal variation is judged less beautiful by average people. Fourth, blemishes matter because they can signal ill health; this, like the principle of symmetry, applies to both sexes. Reddish, moist lips are another sign of youth and health, as well as of sexual arousal.

Finally, and most interestingly, faces—especially women's faces—are preferred if they are more childlike, that is, if they have larger eyes, smaller lower faces, and lighter complexions and hair color. Say what you will about sexism (and most of what you will say is true), there are other reasons for this kind of preference. In every variety of human population, infants and children, relatively speaking, have larger eyes, smaller, lower faces, and lighter complexions and hair color than the adults they are destined to become. Our reaction to these features of infants and children has been called the "cute response," and it has helped ensure their survival. So this fifth dimension of the beauty of faces is a by-product of our built-in reaction to childish ones. When women look at men, this dimension contends with their evolved attraction to men who can protect them from other men; perhaps this is why androgyny sometimes wins over masculinity. When men look at women, there is no such opposition.

Culture plays into these tendencies. Makeup covers blemishes and signs of aging and makes the eyes more prominent so that they seem larger. Some Asians have surgery to make their eyes larger and rounder, some African Americans lighten their skin. Face-lifts and botox injections reverse aging effects. Corsets shift the waist-hip ratio in the desired direction. And so on.

As for noses specifically, not only are they much smaller in infancy and childhood than in adulthood, but they continue to grow throughout life. Making a large nose smaller takes strong cultural advantage of two of the biological tendencies mentioned above. But civilization did not have to wait for the invention of evolutionary psychology to decide that the nose is important.[17] It has been considered the "organ of reputation" since ancient times; cutting it off ensured an enemy or criminal's permanent humiliation, and damage to it was seen as highly important to repair. Physiognomists, who theorized that character could be read from outward appearance, recognized five kinds of noses: the Roman nose was indicative of strength, the Greek of refinement, the pug of weakness and lack of development, the "celestial" of weakness and inquisitiveness, and, last but not least, the

Jewish of (what else?) commercialism. In the early twentieth century, as rhinoplasty was improving and spreading, Jews were able to escape not only the stigma of membership in a despised group but also the imputation of undesirable character traits.

So culture responds, to some extent reflexively, to certain built-in human preferences, but it also acts to counteract or exaggerate them. "Black Is Beautiful," a proud cry of the sixties, may be a less likely cultural choice, but it is a choice human minds are perfectly capable of. And the reverse choice is not just the result of an adaptation in which babies of all ethnic groups are lighter in skin color than the grown-ups they will become; it is also in this case the result of chances of history that happened to make light-skinned people the dominant group in the world for a time. When light-skinned people ruled and dark-skinned people served them—however arbitrary the origins of that arrangement—both rulers and ruled defined darkness downward in value. This cultural process greatly exaggerated any natural tendency that may have preceded it, and if a time comes when darker people rule, "Black Is Beautiful" may become institutionalized.

Something similar can be said about noses. Whatever natural tendency there may be to find a small, childlike nose prettier, domination of Jews by small-nosed people exaggerated it greatly and guaranteed the eventual development of rhinoplasty. Today most Jewish women who seek this surgery are not trying to conceal their ethnicity but to enhance their beauty as—for whatever reason—they see it.

Given the evidence that a nose "out of proportion" to a woman's face is considered unattractive by many cultures, compounded by the fact that small- or straight-nosed people also set the cultural standard, this is not surprising. The operation may be on the rise again among Jews, but they are not alone. In an interesting turn of fate, women in Iran, the nation that at this writing poses the greatest threat to Israel, are having nose jobs in large and growing numbers. In the Middle East, enemies are very often cousins under the skin, and throughout the human family, people like to be and feel beautiful.

14

Bodily Fictions

If nose jobs are a kind of Jewish bodily fiction, they are not the only kind. Not surprisingly, given Jewish anatomical angst, transformations of the body have been a major theme of modern Jewish novels. At their most extreme they are cosmic and comical. In Kafka's *The Metamorphosis*, Gregor Samsa wakes up to find himself changed into a giant insect, so restricted in his movements he cannot even turn over. Yet he has to construct a life, despite a physical form that makes him repulsive, even to himself.

> He was lying on his hard, as it were armor-plated, back and when he lifted his head a little he could see his domelike brown belly divided into stiff arched segments. . . . His numerous legs, which were pitifully thin compared to the rest of his bulk, waved helplessly before his eyes.[1]

After many unsuccessful tries, he manages to get out of bed and open the locked door to admit a clerk from his office, who promptly draws back in horror and heads for the street. Comically, Gregor has the thought that the clerk must not be allowed to leave in this frame of mind—as if that were the main obstacle to his own resumption of bureaucratic duties. But all is not horror and misery. In time "he especially enjoyed hanging suspended from the ceiling . . . one could breathe more freely; one's body swung and rocked lightly." This induced an "almost blissful absorption," which sometimes made him fall, "yet he now had his body much better under control."[2]

But he fears that his harsh and distant father "might take as a piece of peculiar wickedness any excursion of his over the walls or the ceiling,"[3] so his only pleasure is denied him. His father begins pelting him with apples, some sink in, the pain is terrible, and he loses consciousness just as his hysterical mother begs for their son's life.

Alas, one apple rots in his neck—like Adam's, a sign of masculinity? But this causes inflammation, and he dies of it, whereupon his family is liberated to resume normal life. Soon after, "It struck both Mr. and Mrs. Samsa, almost at the same moment, as they became aware of their daughter's increasing vivacity, that in spite of all the sorrow . . . she had bloomed into a pretty girl with a good figure. . . . And it was like a confirmation of their new dreams and excellent intentions that at the end of their journey their daughter sprang to her feet first and stretched her young body."[4] Thus, one lithe and young body is liberated to life, health, and presumably sex by the death of another—a brother—too grotesque to live.

Kafka's father's father had been a kosher butcher, and he was affected by images of his grandfather's hands steeped in flesh and blood. But he was particularly bitter against his father, Hermann, whom he accused in a 1919 letter of turning Franz's bar mitzvah and Passover seders into a nasty farce. In 1914, he had written in his diary, "What have I in common with Jews? I have hardly anything in common with myself and should stand in a corner, content that I can breathe."[5]

This, of course, is exactly what he had in common with Jews. He rejected religion, but at various times avidly embraced Jewish folklore, became obsessed with the Yiddish theater and language, saw his own sickliness (and consequent inability to serve in the German army in World War I) as Jewish, found explicitly Jewish themes in love affairs with Jewish women, learned Hebrew, and contemplated going to Israel. The young Franz had far more in common with Jews than he knew.

In that post-emancipation period between the World Wars, Jews were trying to be like everyone else—to stand in a corner content to breathe—but even this was forbidden. Gregor wakes up an insect, unmasking his pretense of middle-class, bureaucratic normality. In both of his major novels, *The Trial* and *The Castle*—inspired by the vicious anti-Semitism of the Dreyfus affair—protagonists named "K." move uncomprehending and hopeless through a world in which they are fundamentally strangers, and which has no use for them.

In "A Hunger Artist," the protagonist starves himself for forty days at a time to fascinate the clients at a circus menagerie, always tempted to fast a little longer against the advice of his impresario, who at the end turns him over to interested ladies ready to care for him: "The artist now submitted completely . . . his body was hollowed out; his legs in a spasm of self-preservation . . . scraped on the ground as if it were not really solid ground; and the whole weight of his body . . . relapsed onto one of the ladies, who, looking around for help and panting a little . . . to the great delight of the spectators burst into tears and had to be replaced by an attendant who had long been stationed in readiness."[6] An almost sexual fascination, for the gentle ladies, turns into disgust, as they realize they are dealing with pathological suffering. The "Jewish" weakness that kept Kafka out of the army here extends to the vanishing point.

None of this can be separated from Kafka's sad sense of himself as a Jew, forever the suffering outsider trying to blend in, yet demanding attention and—always ambivalently—an end to his suffering. To be sure, these alienated, deformed, suffering men can be seen as writers, or simply as human beings. But in fact Kafka *was* Jewish and locked in a lifelong struggle with his Jewishness, in a time and place when Jewishness was about to become the world's most dangerous deformity.

Most poignant, perhaps, is "Report to an Academy." In this wondrous fable, an ape who has been forced to become human gives an audience of scientists a first-person account. He tells of being shot and captured (a hip wound gives him a permanent limp, just like Jacob after besting the angel), unwillingly trained away from his real self, and thoroughly contemptuous of the moral aspect of the change: "I repeat:

there was no attraction for me in imitating human beings; I imitated them because I needed a way out, and for no other reason."[7] It happens just after he utters his first word— "Hallo!"—which he belches out in a drunken stupor while learning to drink schnapps. If this is the ape's view of the human world he is forced to join, it is also the Jew's view of the Gentile world he is trained to mimic, and it entails the same moral outrage of self-suppression.

The Metamorphosis has had many echoes. In Philip Roth's version, the transformation of David Kepesh is "a massive hormonal influx" or "an endocrinopathic catastrophe."[8] The result? "I am a breast . . . a mammary gland disconnected from any human form . . . an organism with the general shape of a football . . . of a spongy consistency. . . ." Most of his body had turned to fat, and he had taken on an almost round shape except for a nipple at the top that was once his head. This extension had seventeen holes, basically milk ducts, "each about half the size of the male urethral orifice."

In addition, there is a telling feature that connects his present grotesque appearance to what seems to be its point of origin: "My nipple is rosy pink in color—as was the stain I had discovered at the base of my penis stepping into the shower the night this all happened to me." Unlike Gregor's transformation, David's is thoroughly sexual. It begins with "a mild, sporadic tingling in the groin" and soon progresses to discoloration, "as though a small raspberry, or maybe a cherry" had been crushed at the base of his penis, making its root "unmistakably *red*."[9] In fact, the lead-up to this remarkable illness is a bizarre and sudden hypersexuality. After a year of complete erotic boredom with his lovely wife, he becomes almost insanely passionate about her overnight:

> Sex, not in the head, not in the heart, but excruciatingly in the epidermis of the penis . . . I found myself writhing with pleasure, clawing at the sheets. . . . I took Claire's ear in my mouth and licked it like a dog. I licked her hair. I found myself, panting, licking my own shoulder. . . . "Is this what is meant by debauchery?" I asked my happy friend. . . . She only smiled.[10]

The payback for unbridled maleness seems to be to have your identity sunk into a shapeless, pudgy breast. One day in the hospital a nurse is washing him and it gives him a burning sensation. "I'm only washing your face." "My face? Where is my face! Where are my arms! My legs! Where is my mouth! What happened to me!"[11] Like Gregor, he has lost his body, and what he has gained in its stead is both impotent and disgusting.

Yet it is somehow physically, even sexually lush, the exaggeration of a bodily appetite until it becomes insufferably embodied; Gregor's exoskeleton is disgusting, too, but it is a dry sort of grotesquerie, the result of a failure to really live. While David's raspberry or cherry is the lightning that heralds a hormonal storm, Gregor is killed by a sexual apple, sinking into his dry body and festering into poison.

The Hunger Artist is more like Gregor, transforming

himself and shriveling into disembodied nothing from *lack* of appetite. Explaining himself with his last breath, pursing his lips as if for a kiss, he whispers "right into the overseer's ear, so that no syllable might be lost, 'because I couldn't find the food I liked. If I had found it, believe me, I should have made no fuss and stuffed myself like you or anyone else' . . . 'Well, clear this out now!' said the overseer, and they buried the hunger artist, straw and all."[12]

Into the vacant cage, they put a young panther, and "even the most insensitive" spectators "felt it refreshing to see this wild creature leaping around. . . . The panther was all right. The food he liked was brought him . . . his noble body, furnished to the bursting point with all that it needed, seemed to carry freedom around with it too; somewhere in his jaws it seemed to lurk; and the joy of life streamed with such ardent passion from his throat that for the onlookers it was not easy to stand. . . . But they braced themselves, crowded around the cage, and did not ever want to move away."[13]

Like *The Metamorphosis*, which ends with a lithe young body bursting with life, the closing words of "A Hunger Artist" tell us that on the rare occasions when average people see a really *living* creature they are shocked but riveted. David, in contrast, is transformed by too much life, too much hunger too fully satisfied. Having found the "food" he likes, he gorges on it until it becomes him. These polar opposites, both paths to the anatomical grotesque, evoke the Scylla and Charybdis of anti-Semitic caricatures of Jews: They have either too much or too little body, are one day emasculated (overcircumcised?) eunuchs of bourse and study hall, the next hypersexual monsters threatening Christian virgins; either way they grow grotesque and can't win for losing.

Unlike Gregor's tyrannical father, David's is "a great and noble man," a former short-order cook who became the proprietor of a classic hotel in the Catskills, an area where New York Jews summered for generations. (You might say he indulged Jewish appetites when they let themselves go.) An ordinary Jew immersed in a Jewish world, he has the strength to sit with "Davey" in his dreadful condition and concoct compassionate small talk. Yet his father no longer kisses him.

As for his mother, "Mercifully for her she is dead; if she wasn't, this would have killed her."[14] His wife, whose life has gone from the sexually sublime to the medically ridiculous, rises to the crisis as best she can, but in the end he is alone in his tragicomedy, a prisoner of unpitying hormones. But there is symmetry: The hormones that once drove his way with women (and still drive his fantasies) have turned on him; his lust for breasts has made him one.

Report to an Academy" suggests that a Jew can be forced to replace his own language with another and even to change his bodily form, but he will do it only under duress and after being made drunk by his captors—in other words, forcibly and unconscionably. Kafka's ape (or Jew) can be made human only through subterfuge, a harsh sidelight on the ethical foundations of humanity.

Certainly the immorality of Europe's treatment of Jews was coming to a head and would soon enough present Jewish writers with perhaps the greatest challenge any artists have faced. Several great Jewish writers visualized that horror as the ultimate transformation of the body—into nothing. Paul Celan's great poem "*Todesfuge*"—"Death Fugue"—is a chillingly beautiful evocation of Auschwitz, repeatedly contrasting the appearance of two prototypical girls: *dein goldenes haar Margareta / dein aschenes haar Sulamit*—your golden hair Margareta / your ashen hair Shulamit. But the poem also disembodies the murdered Jews. In John Felstiner's translation,[15] "you'll rise then as smoke to the sky / you'll have a grave then in the clouds there you won't lie too cramped." Primo Levi, the great Italian-Jewish writer who also survived the Holocaust for a time, said of "*Todesfuge*," "I carry it within me like a graft,"[16] and in his own novel *If Not Now, When?*, the song of the partisans quotes it, saying that the murdered Jews "have dug themselves a grave in the air."[17] Celan and Levi both killed themselves many years after the war; Hitler's epoch may have been survivable, but what they carried away from it was not.

Avraham Sutzkever, perhaps the greatest Yiddish poet, wrote a poem to his murdered baby son that turned the boy into something almost as insubstantial as smoke and clouds, but much more positive, echoing the fundamental Jewish dust-to-dust expectation and hope:

> I will let you slip
> into the beckoning snow . . .
> and you will sink
> a sunset sliver
> into its still and deep
> and bear my greeting up
> into the frosty shoots of grass[18]

And Cynthia Ozick, writing decades later about what she fortunately did not directly experience, powerfully evoked the imagined transformation of another murdered baby, as seen by the baby's grief-stricken mother:

> Far off, very far, Magda leaned across her air-fed belly, reaching out with the rods of her arms. She was high up, elevated, riding someone's shoulder. But the shoulder that carried Magda . . . was drifting away, the speck of Magda was moving more and more into the smoky distance. Above the shoulder a helmet glinted.[19]

The wearer of the helmet throws the baby against the electrified fence of the death camp. "How far Magda was from Rosa now. . . . She was no bigger than a moth! All at once Magda was swimming through the air. The whole of Magda traveled through loftiness. She looked like a butterfly touching a silver vine."

This story, "The Shawl," has a long aching echo in the novella *Rosa*, in which Ozick's continuing fascination with physical transformation is directed, both painfully and comically, at the aging of Magda's lonely mother, who has concocted a whole history and adult life for her dead girl and writes to her regularly. She gets "hit on" in the Laundromat by a seventy-one-year-old fellow retiree—"with his false teeth and his dewlaps and his rakehell reddish toupee"—but by the time they get to the cafeteria (Kollins Kosher Kameo) she is exhausted: "Rosa looked in the window. Her bun was loose, strings dangling on either side of her neck. The reflection of a ragged old bird with worn feathers. Skinny, a stork." At their table,

> she sat and panted. . . . Everyone had canes, dowager's humps, acrylic teeth, shoes cut out for bunions . . . an open collar showing mottled skin, ferocious clavicles, the wrinkled foundations of wasted breasts. . . . [S]he felt the cooling sweat licking from around her neck down her spine into the crevice of her bottom. She was afraid to shift. . . . If she moved even a little, an odor would fly up: urine, salt, old woman's fatigue. She left off panting and shivered. What do I care? I'm used to everything.[20]

Magda is now, in her mother's mind, a married young woman as real as can be: "Forgive me, my yellow lioness," one letter opens and goes on to call her "my snow queen." It ends, "In me the strength of your being consumes my joy. Yellow blossom! Cup of the sun!" Magda has no body, yet her mother is almost all body, and decrepit body at that. Still, she is no weakling. She is in Florida because she personally—"part with a big hammer . . . part with a piece of construction metal I picked up in the gutter"—and single-handedly demolished her own secondhand furniture store. And she can summon her murdered daughter at will:

> The whole room was full of Magda: she was like a butterfly. . . . Rosa waited to see what age Magda was going to be: how nice, a girl of sixteen . . . all in flower . . . Magda's hair was still as yellow as buttercups, and so slippery and fine that her two barrettes . . . kept sliding down toward the sides of her chin—that chin which was the marvel of her face . . . The jaw was ever so slightly too long, a deepened oval, so that her mouth, especially the lower lip, was not crowded but rather made a definite mark in the middle of spaciousness. Consequently the mouth seemed as significant as a body arrested in orbit, and Magda's sky-filled eyes, nearly rectangular at the corners, were like two obeisant satellites.[21]

She builds Magda's face out of airy nothing, and it is strangely beautiful.

Still, Rosa lets the lovely Magda go away when her septuagenarian suitor calls, supplanting the post-Holocaust idyll with an aged, ugly, ridiculous, yet strikingly alive embrace of the real, replacing the disembodied fantasy with a pair of real, moldering, malodorous bodies. Yet Magda is no less real to her than the suitor or herself, and together they make an almost coherent narrative of the body and how it betrays us—more slowly but just as surely as Gregor's betrayed him—a narrative of physicality, of weakness punc-

tuated by bursts of strength and lingering sexuality, a narrative deeply Jewish and deeply human.

In Isaac Bashevis Singer's great works of fiction, all composed in Yiddish, transformations of the body and of the
soul are intertwined. In *Satan in Goray*, a badly abused young
woman in the mid 1600s—a time of massacres, false messi-
ahs, and upheaval throughout Europe—is possessed by a
dybbuk, an agent of the Devil, and becomes a threat to her
Jewish community until it is exorcised. She dies exhausted
by her ordeal, her body unable to survive this spiritual
treachery.

In contrast, in the almost comical work *The Magician of
Lublin*, a seemingly normal Jew has a secret life as a magician. This involves constant transformation and miraculous
Houdini-like escapes—professional secrets—but he also has
four girlfriends and a wife, and juggling them involves some
secrets, too. At last, by some ineffable ultimate magic, he
morphs himself into a good Jew again.

In the marvelous "Taibele and Her Demon," no real
demons appear, but a strange and imaginative man changes
into one—sort of.[22] Taibele is an abandoned wife, an almost
irremediable condition for a religious Jew; her husband has
left her after all three of their children have died, and she
may not marry until he is found dead or alive. Alchonon, an
impoverished teacher's helper, overhears her one night talking to a friend about a storybook in which a young Jewish

woman is ravished by a demon. The eavesdropper sneaks into Taibele's bedroom, claiming to be the nephew of Asmodeus, King of the Demons, and tells her that her husband is dead. "Since he was a demon and not a man, Taibele returned his kisses and moistened his beard with her tears. Evil spirit though he was, he treated her kindly."

In an ironic pretense of transformation, he tells her that he has abandoned his real, demonic body and made himself look like a man, so that she shouldn't die of fright. This "demon" visits her twice a week for years, having his way with her yet showing her great tenderness and thoroughly enchanting her with wild tales of the demons' world. He claims to have seven other wives, all she-devils, and describes them in detail.

Taibele comes to love him, and although he dies without revealing who he is, he has transformed her life and his own by a bizarre, humane subterfuge—the kind of sexual trickery that peppers the Jewish Bible, often with positive outcomes. She attends the real Alchonon's funeral but doesn't make the connection, simply mourning their respective lonely lives; yet they have for many years healed one another's loneliness. In this and in much of Singer's other fiction, sex is embodied and miraculous, false and true, selfish and selfless, destructive and redemptive, as in life.

Nonsexual physical prowess has also been a theme, although (as in the Bible) sexual prowess may not be far behind. In Saul Bellow's *Henderson the Rain King*, the title character, a huge man with almost superhuman strength, fights a war, builds a farm where he trusses and slaughters pigs with his bare hands, and goes to Africa on a whim, where by hefting a huge stone idol no one else can lift he becomes the successor to a tribal king, required to service all the king's many wives. In Bernard Malamud's *The Natural*, the greatest baseball player who ever lived—he is almost magical—is shot in the stomach by a crazy woman and put out of baseball for twenty years. But he returns, by the game's standards a very old man, triumphantly finding the power and strength to win for his team even as his old wound opens up and his life bleeds out of him, while his son watches.

But neither of these heroes is Jewish, and that is very unusual for both novelists. Bellow's and Malamud's books are mostly about what another gifted writer, Joseph Epstein, has called "fabulous small Jews." In Bellow's case they are mostly wry, self-absorbed intellectuals who have trouble taking action; in Malamud's they are an assortment of merchants, writers, and others—one the famous victim of a Russian blood libel—who seem more acted upon than acting. In a sense, *Henderson* and *The Natural* are about golems, non-Jewish creatures created by writer-rabbis to perform acts of superhuman (certainly super-Jewish) strength, the breath breathed into them by secular sages.

The other secular sage, Philip Roth, is also the comic poet laureate of the Jewish body, not just or even mainly because of *The Breast*. From *Goodbye, Columbus*, with its details of Brenda Patimkin's deliciously athletic (albeit nearsighted)

Jewish body through *Sabbath's Theater*, whose middle-aged protagonist masturbates (reverentially) on his dead lover's grave, and beyond, to *Everyman* and *Exit Ghost*, in which old and sick protagonists lust vainly after pretty young women who are themselves the picture of health, Roth has relentlessly chronicled Jewish sexual physicality.

But in *Portnoy's Complaint*, his comedic art soared. One of the most embodied Jewish novels, it is an anguished Rabelaisian riff on the Jewish body. And it's not just about sex; the narrator supplies many painful details of his father's heroic struggles with his unmovable bowels, as well as his mother's struggles with her only son over what he doesn't eat. She famously brandishes a long knife at him to make him eat dinner, a scene that became, regrettably, emblematic of Jewish motherhood.

Self-loathing, in part projected onto his cartoon parents, is a deeply motivating force for Portnoy. But although he wants us to believe that he would thoroughly love his body had they not prevented him, we know better; the body offers enough to complain about whether or not our parents try to turn us against it. Aging, disease, injury, natural weakness, unpleasant odors, and, for that matter, longing, anger, fear, and grief grasp at every normal, feeble human body, often in an untimely way, regardless of what we have been taught—by Jewish or any culture.

But sexual anatomy is at the heart of the comedy. One of the three meanings of the title—the medical one—is literally fleshed out in the epigraph, which defines the syndrome as a psychosexual ailment traceable to the mother-child relationship. The narrator speaks the book entirely to his analyst, sometimes addressing him as "Doctor," but although there is a light drumbeat of psychoanalytic theory throughout the book, Portnoy's own view is much more practical.

The story and characters are thoroughly Jewish, the book peppered with Yiddish; the French translation I picked up in a stall in an open weekly market in the small village of Cessenon-sur-Orb has a glossary of Yiddish words and phrases, most of which would not be known to American readers either. The narrator and the doctor are both Jewish, as is of course this caricature of a family. The ex-lax-abusing father who spends half his life on the toilet and who can't hold a baseball bat properly, the oxymoronic knife-wielding I'll-kill-you-if-you-don't-eat mother with seductive legs in perfumed stockings—all this and more is, at least in the narrator's mind, distinctively Jewish. All around him call attention to their identity and he is sick of it: "Jew Jew Jew Jew Jew Jew! It is coming out of my ears already, the saga of the suffering Jews! Do me a favor my people, and stick your suffering heritage up your suffering ass—*I happen also to be a human being!*"[3] Although the Holocaust is at the moment under way, the boy of course wants a normal life.

This particular human being happens also to be hypersexual from bar mitzvah age, when he begins to masturbate at every hour of the day or night, in every imaginable venue, into every conceivable receptacle except a woman's body. "Through a world of matted handkerchiefs and crumpled Kleenex and stained pajamas, I moved my raw and swollen penis." There was also a Mound's candy wrapper, a cored apple, and, most famously, a slab of raw calf's liver from his mother's refrigerator, "rolled around my cock in the bathroom at three-thirty—and . . . again on the end of a fork, at five-thirty."[24] He had done a piece of liver before, bought with his own pocket change, behind a billboard on the way to a bar mitzvah lesson: "I fucked my own family's dinner." The gross violation of Jewish laws about the purity of food is pointed enough, but the slap in his mother's face is almost audible.

He is soon enough doing the same to women (the fuck as well as the figurative slap), but only shiksas—some from the best WASP families, but one a coal-miner's-daughter-turned-fashion-model. She can barely read and write but, in addition to being perfect in face and form, is the most sexually gifted woman on the planet. At first his prominent Jewish "shnoz" holds him back, but when he finds out the Gentile women like him *because* he's Jewish, he plows through them with abandon. However, when he makes the mistake of chasing Jewish women in the Jewish homeland, he is impotent not once but twice, first with a "a young woman with green eyes and tawny hair who is a lieutenant in the Jewish army . . . her small, voluptuous figure nipped at the middle by . . . her khaki belt,"[25] then with a former soldier girl, a kibbutznik, who physically fights him off when he tries to rape her, all while she continues reviling his bourgeois Jewish-Diaspora softness. Using Israeli army tactics, she overpowers him for a while, but ultimately he pins her with his superior weight and promptly loses his erection.

"Doctor: *I couldn't get it up in the State of Israel!* How's that for symbolism, *bubi?*"

But this is not the main lament (the second meaning of "complaint") that he directs to his analyst. "Doctor, my doctor, what do you say, LET'S PUT THE ID BACK IN YID! Liberate this nice Jewish boy's libido, will you please? Raise the prices if you have to—I'll pay anything!"[26] He has, he believes, been relentlessly impaired in his ability to enjoy his body by having had a Jewish—read *repressive*—childhood. Non-Jewish women of any stripe can arouse him, but American Jewish women are too much like his mother, while Israeli women unman him because they are more man than he is. They are the female muscle-Jews, purified by generations of land and war; he is the classic feminized European Diaspora Jew made only more ridiculous in America, severed from tradition, fantasizing about manhood but hopelessly lost in the puerile sexuality of a middle-aged bar mitzvah boy. In time-honored Diaspora fashion, he tries to buy his way out of his body, but in the book's last line the doctor only says, "So . . . Now vee may perhaps to begin. Yes?"

The English novelist Clive Sinclair's short story "Wingate Football Club" begins by telling us that the title team is the only Jewish one in the London football league, and that against all probability they once won the London League Cup. Named after Orde Wingate, the British officer who helped train Israel's early self-defense force ("our version of

Lawrence . . . a *goyisher* Zionist"), the team has spent most seasons near the bottom, but somehow this year they get to the Cup Final.

Like Barney Ross's fights, the game and the spectators are thick with ethnic rivalry. The narrator, a Jewish boy, calls one player "the quicksilver Jewboy," one well-dressed spectator "the Prince of Schmattes." But when the game ends with Wingate winning, "As the whistle blew a woman in a fake leopard-skin coat said out loud, 'Hitler was right! Send the Jews to the showers!' " A teenage boy nearby calls her a bitch, she slaps his face, he hits her back, she calls him a dirty Jew, and her huge companion starts hitting the youth until Al Pinsky intervenes.

"Now Al wasn't tall, so that golem just laughed," but Pinsky was once lightweight champion of Britain. "The golem dropped the boy and took a swing at Pinsky. His fists were the size of hams. Pinsky ducked, like he was taking a bow, then straightened up and calmly knocked the fellow cold."

These simultaneous victories inspire the narrator to try out for the football team at boarding school, where the coach is skeptical until he watches him. " 'Not bad,' he said, 'I didn't think your people liked physical activity. . . . I bet your father earns a lot of money, eh?' " But another boy, Solomon, is fearful, plays badly, and gets no mercy. When he refuses to run with the ball at a line of scary teammates, the coach hits him "hard round the head. 'You have no choice, you greasy tub of chopped liver.' " He runs at the other boys who, following coach's lead, beat him up and make him cry.

Later, at university, the narrator's sexuality is fully awakened by Linda, the self-styled "most experienced virgin in the Western hemisphere," who gives him a bellyache from frustration. She also awakens his admiration for Israel—he meets her at the Jewish and Israel Society—especially during the Six-Day War, which makes him recall something the Prince of Schmattes said to him at the Wingate game about playing to win: " 'We Jews have always been too fussy. When did pussyfooting around ever get us anywhere?' " He tries to go, to help in any way, but the war ends too soon, so he and Linda watch it on television: "Films showed tanks scooting over the Sinai desert. . . . Soldiers hugged and kissed beneath the Western Wall . . . looking like they had just scored the winning goal. . . . I had not felt such exultation since Wingate took the London League Cup."

He and Linda marry and honeymoon there, where soft little Solomon, the "tub of chopped liver," has become Israeli and fought in the war. "He was no longer the weedy Yid of our school-days. . . . A man among men, a real Yiddisher *mensch*." When Linda gets into a shouting match with some Jewish yahoos after a movie ("Four Esaus, looking for a fight"), little Solomon defends her honor, defeating all of them. It turns out he's the lightweight wrestling champion of the army.

This skill sends him to the Munich Olympics, but it is no match for Palestinian terrorists. "Solomon could not wrestle with men holding machine-guns; his skills were trumped, he was as helpless as a schoolboy again." The ending retells the tale of the Jewish body: Jews yearn for physical strength to reverse millennial weakness and the searing contempt of the strong; a soft, scared Jewish body morphs into a warrior-champion; and bodily strength alone is found ultimately trivial in the face of new technologies, which must at last stand in for bodily strength—it is rifles, tanks, and planes that win in the end, not muscle alone. But, finally, Israeli Jews have both. Solomon's murder leaves his grieving friends set on aliyah. "I want any child of mine to be born in Israel," the story concludes, "*L'shanah haba-ah birushalayim*. Next year in Jerusalem."

15

Jewish Power

As far back as the first Jewish literary work, the Torah, we are told that Jews relied on God for power. One of the best-known Hebrew phrases among non-Hebrew-speaking Jews is *b'yad chazakah u'vizroa netuyah*—with a strong hand and an outstretched arm. It is repeated every year during the seder at Passover, the most widely celebrated of Jewish holidays: "The Lord took us out of Egypt with a strong hand and an outstretched arm, and with a great manifestation, and with signs and wonders."

The germ of this cherished and time-worn sentence lies in an interesting context. It is Exodus, chapter 6, the Torah portion known to Jews as *Va'era*—"*I appeared*." It is God who is speaking, and in answer to the most insolent challenge tossed at Him by one of his lieutenants since Abraham tried to teach God about justice and why Sodom and Gomorrah should not be crushed. Moses is the source of the challenge this time and he is, if anything, more insolent than Abraham. He doesn't even apologize.

He is smarting from a bitter confrontation he has had with the Hebrew slaves, whose work has been made much harder by Pharaoh's response to Moses's (and God's) demand to let his people go. Formerly given straw to make into bricks, they now have to scatter over the landscape and gather their own straw, yet produce the same quota of bricks. Moses (and God) have taken their aching bodies and burdened them to the breaking point. They ask God to punish not Pharaoh but Moses, for "putting a sword in their hands to slay us" (Exod. 5:21).[1]

So there is more than a little reflected bitterness when Moses says, "O Lord, why did You bring harm upon this people? Why did You send me? Ever since I came to Pharaoh to speak in Your name, he has dealt worse with this people; and still You have not delivered Your people" (Exod. 5:22–23). The response is prompt and decisive: *Now you will see what I will do to Pharaoh*. It is almost as if God has been waiting for Moses to prove himself with righteous anger. In the King James Version: "With a strong hand shall he let them go, and with a strong hand shall he drive them out of his land" (Exod. 6:13). God continues: "And I appeared unto Abraham, unto Isaac, and unto Jacob . . . I have also heard the groaning of the children of Israel . . . and I have remembered my covenant. Wherefore say unto the children of Israel, I am the Lord, and I will bring you out from under the burdens of the Egyptians . . . I will redeem you with a stretched out arm" (Exod. 6:3–6).[2]

The outstretched arm of the unembodied God fights battles with and for the Jews from that point forward. After leading the people across the sea and watching the Egyptian army drown, Moses sings, "The Lord is a man of war. . . .

Pharaoh's chariots and his army He has cast into the sea. . . . Your right hand, O Lord, shatters the foe! . . . At the blast of Your nostrils the waters piled up. . . . You put out Your right hand, the earth swallowed them" (Exod. 15:3–10).[3]

This Song of Moses, now part of the Sabbath morning service, prefigures other wars to come: "The peoples hear, they tremble; agony grips the dwellers in Philistia. Now are the clans of Edom dismayed; The tribes of Moab—trembling grips them; all the dwellers in Canaan are aghast" (Exod. 15:14–15). And indeed the Egyptians are only the first enemies of the Jews against whom the Lord raises a strong hand. In Deuteronomy, chapter 20, the Lord "marches with you to do battle for you against your enemy, to bring you victory" (v. 4).

In Judges, chapter 7, we have the strange spectacle of God telling Gideon to get rid of most of his troops: " 'You have too many troops with you for Me to deliver Midian into their hands; Israel might claim for themselves the glory due to Me" (v. 2). In Psalm 18, God "trained my hands for battle" (v. 34) and "brought my adversaries low before me" (v. 40). Psalm 24 defines the King of glory as "the Lord mighty and valiant, the Lord valiant in battle" (v. 8).

There is no reason to think that these and many other similar references were to the ancient Hebrews the sorts of metaphoric statements we find in them today. Indeed, there is every reason to believe that the Hebrews and the Jews who stemmed from them took the most literal meaning from these words. And if this applied to the time before the Romans destroyed Judea, when Jews fought fiercely with

God beside them, it applied even more strongly to the Diaspora, when they often could not fight for themselves at all and became accustomed to relying on God alone to protect them against their very real enemies. So in the Diaspora they cultivated other forms of power, with the goal not of victory but of survival.

Rarely has this power been as eloquently and succinctly described as in an article by Mark Twain, "Concerning the Jews," that appeared in *Harper's Monthly* in 1898. It was spurred by the increasingly vicious anti-Semitism he had seen on his recent European travels. He wrote of the Dreyfus trial and the growing movement to expel the Jews from Germany. But he ended this way: "Jews constitute but one percent of the human race. It suggests a nebulous, dim puff of star dust lost in the blaze of the Milky Way. Properly the Jew ought hardly to be heard of; but he is heard of, has always been heard of. He is as prominent on the planet as any other people, and his commercial importance is extravagantly out of proportion to the smallness of his bulk. His contributions to the world's list of great names in literature, science, art, music, finance, medicine and abstruse learning are also way out of proportion to the smallness of his numbers. He has made a marvelous fight in this world, in all ages; and has done it with his hands tied behind him."

This was in 1898, before Jews had won 155 Nobel Prizes. He describes empires that "sit in twilight now, or have vanished. The Jew saw them all, beat them all, and is now what he always was, exhibiting no decadence, no infirmities of age, no weakening of his parts, no slowing of his energies, no dulling of his alert and aggressive mind. All things are mortal but the Jew; all other forces pass, but he remains." Alas, Jews would soon prove mortal enough.

It was mind he had emphasized in the article, but as he later wrote of it, "I was ignorant—like the rest of the Christian world—of the fact that the Jew had a record as a soldier. . . . I find that he furnished soldiers and high officers to the Revolution, the War of 1812, and the Mexican War. In the Civil War he was represented in the armies and navies of both the North and the South by 10 per cent of his numerical strength—the same percentage that was furnished by the Christian populations. . . . His record for capacity, for fidelity, and for gallant soldiership in the field is as good as any one's."

Twain's prescience becomes almost preternatural when he writes that the Jews are active in politics, but "scatter their work and their votes . . . lose the advantages to be had by concentration." He goes on with wry humor: "Dr. Herzl . . . wishes to gather the Jews of the world together in Palestine, with a government of their own. . . . I am not objecting; but . . . I think it would be politic to stop it. It will not be well to let the race find out its strength. If the horses knew theirs, we should not ride any more." In the end they did gather into their own land, where they indeed found out their strength, and no one rides them anymore.

What Twain did not understand—what even Herzl did not understand—was that the strength they had to find was not just spiritual, scientific, literary, and commercial, but muscular and martial; more Apollonian than Dionysian to be sure, but still much more Greek, or at least more Hebrew, than Jewish. In other words, they had to bring to a close almost two millennia in which they literally expected the strong hand and outstretched arm of their cherished God to fight their battles not just with but for them. Events that neither Twain nor Herzl lived to see showed them, perhaps, that God expects them to help themselves—to gird themselves for real, physical fighting.

And so they built their bodily and military strength to back up the spiritual, intellectual, and commercial power they had long wielded. God, they now believe, may be beside them but will not go before them, nor take their place in the new annals of war. So once again they fight to keep part of their ancient land for themselves. Many of them hope that God will help them, but they are not waiting for God. The strong hand and outstretched arm they rely on first and foremost is their own.

B ut of course they are not safe. After the bombing of a Jerusalem pizzeria in 2001, the columnist George Will wrote in the *Washington Post*, "Israel needs a short war and a high wall." He quoted *USA Today*'s Jack Kelley, an eyewitness:

The blast . . . sent flesh flying onto second-story balconies a block away. Three men were blown 30 feet;

their heads, separated from their bodies by the blast, rolled down the glass-strewn street. . . . One woman had at least six nails embedded in her neck. . . . A man groaned. . . . His legs were blown off. Blood poured from his torso. . . . A 3-year-old girl, her face covered with glass, walked among the bodies calling her mother's name. . . . One rabbi found a small hand against a white Subaru parked outside the restaurant.

Six of the fifteen killed were children; until the security fence was built, this was done repeatedly. Palestinians have lost children, too, but as Will observed, the Israeli children "were not collateral victims—they were the targets. Abdullah Shami, a senior official of Islamic Jihad, celebrated 'this successful operation' against 'pigs and monkeys.' " Shami's view was broadcast on the official television station of Yasir Arafat's Palestinian Authority: " 'All weapons must be aimed at Jews. . . . Blessings to he who shot a bullet into the head of a Jew.' "

The Palestinians need and deserve a state of their own, and they will get one, if and as they accept a Jewish presence in the ancient Jewish homeland. Jewish bodies in uniform have been used for some interesting purposes over the years. In 1982, they dragged Jewish settlers out of a settlement in the Sinai, and that oil-rich territory gained at great cost in Israeli blood and treasure was returned to Egypt in exchange for peace. In 2005, Jewish soldiers dragged other Jews out of settlements in the Gaza Strip, a major gesture toward a two-state solution. The result has been a relentless rain of rockets from Gaza onto towns inside Israel, a Palestinian civil war within Gaza, and a takeover of Gaza by Hamas terrorists; and yet the peace process has resumed.

These actions of Israel's soldiers point to what it will do when it has a partner for peace on the Palestinian side. When the time comes, Jewish soldiers will once again use force to drag unwilling Jewish bodies—perhaps going limp in passive resistance, perhaps raising arms against their own people's soldiers—out of lands won at great sacrifice, which will then become a Palestinian state. The fact that these West Bank lands are the heart of biblical Israel will not make this easier, but it will be done.

Meanwhile, the world must understand that the Holocaust is not a distant memory for Jews; it occurred only yesterday, the blink of an eye in the course of history. Enemies of the Jewish people naturally choose to deny it, forget it, or, more subtly, minimize its importance and criticize Jews for making too much of it. Another specious claim is that it has little to do with the Middle East, a mistake even Palestinian historians don't make. The world owes Israel to the Jews. It belonged to them from time immemorial; they were forced out by Western power, and at last Western power approved of their return. They are there to stay.

Couldn't Iranian nuclear bombs kill millions of Israelis? Certainly, but then all of Iran's cities and towns will be turned to radioactive rubble, a terrible symmetry just like the one that prevented war between the United States and the Soviet Union for over forty years. Physical strength, as Israeli wrestlers found at the Munich Olympics, can't

Jewish child survivors of the Holocaust being sent back
to Hamburg, Germany, after attempting to land
at Haifa, Israel, in 1947 on the ship *Exodus*.
Keystone/Hulton Archive. Used by permission of Getty Images.

always, ultimately protect you, but it can make people afraid
of you, and that in itself is protection; *so that where the respect
cannot be won by entreaty, it may be commanded, and where it cannot be commanded, it may be enforced.*

Many survivors did make it to Israel, and they have
been called "the seventh million," not just to memo-
rialize six million murdered Jews but to signify their impact
on the character of the state. This was not always admitted
by the pioneers, who wanted pure labor Zionism to be the
state's only motive force.

But in the end the hardy farmers and soldiers of the early

twentieth century blended in unpredicted ways with the ragtag horde of Nazi victims, starved stragglers forced immediately to fight six invading Arab armies. One common goal they set with no dispute: *Never again.* They brought up new generations who above all were not raised to be victims.

These new Jewish children would sometimes ask how six million Jews could die without fighting back. They were told of the episodes of heroic resistance but mostly were taught that the Jews of Europe had not been trained to fight, while they would be. Their fears and their confusion were treated with bracing medicine: three years in the army honing their bodies, mastering weapons, becoming warriors. They visited Yad Vashem, Israel's Holocaust memorial, lit a candle, said a prayer, maybe wept a little. Then they went off to put their bodies on the line, to defend their homes and families as most Jews had not been allowed to do for centuries. And they answered their own question: *We are different.* They were a new kind of Jew who would impose such costs on future persecutors as none of their past enemies dreamed of.

16

Deborah's Daughters

Portnoy's complaints about them aside, women were central to the Zionist enterprise from the first modern wave of immigration, and without their bodies on the line there would have been no Israel. In 1889, one wrote, "I still yearn for Russia. The heat and the khamsin (the desert wind) are very difficult . . . in the winter it is raining, and this is the best time of the entire year. . . . The winter season here is full of different types of vegetables and fruit. . . . It is possible to live well here if God grants health and strength!"[1] God did not always oblige. "The change in climate affected me badly, and on the fifth day after my arrival I got sick with malaria, God forbid, and I lay in bed for eight days. . . . Every foreigner who comes to live here from a faraway land has to drink from this cup, no one is spared."

A quarter-century later, another woman doubted the experiment. "As early as 1881–1882, a pioneering, wonderful, idealistic type of person came to Palestine. . . . And now, after they spent 25 years in the country, we found them completely reliant on the officials, lacking any faith in their enterprise, and employing Arab workers. They were all bitter and hopeless. . . . Their sons did not continue in the farms and left the country because they could not stand the work regime."[2]

Yet the kibbutz movement was then just beginning in earnest—and not a moment too soon, since a new hardening was needed from both sexes. The physical challenges changed little. A 1912 diary entry by a woman named Anya:

We lead a curious life here. I do the same work every day. It is very boring. In the morning, as soon as I get up, I must stoke the stove, then boil the milk, peel the potatoes for the stew and cook some soup. . . . Then I must do the dishes and sweep the room. And rest for a while. Then the Samovar again, dinner, the dishes, fatigue and sleep. And the next day, it's the same thing all over again. The hands are always dirty. I wash them and feel sad because they are getting so rough. . . . There are eight of us now, six men, one other girl and myself. One of our comrades died last week. He was simple, and gentle and open-eyed. Very sweet and good, alive and practical, a young man of twenty-four or five. We are not yet joined together. There are mis-understandings. We are all so different. I am often ill with Malaria. The climate here is not healthy. I gain weight and then grow thin suddenly. They say one must hope for better times, but I do not believe all this. The entire settlement, the entire region, is infected with Cholera. . . . It is late now. . . . I must get up early tomorrow.[3]

B ut another young woman in 1925 felt the dream being realized in her body. "I am happy to be free, to have regained my energy and warmth, and to feel the firm ground under my feet. . . . I have been associated with the kibbutz movement for several years, but I only now comprehend its depth, and the beauty of going together with other people . . . who strive for a better future. I am not blinded. I can see the negative aspects of our life. . . . I am happy because I love the kibbutz and have such faith in its way. . . . I would like to help all those who can understand our truth—who can find a way to us."[4] Millions did.

O ne, Hannah Senesh, didn't stay. She, too, loved her kibbutz and was scarcely daunted by its intense physical challenges. But World War II was raging, and she joined a group who volunteered to be dropped behind German lines to try to save Jews; she was captured, tortured, and hanged.[5]

She was one of a new breed. Vitka Kempner, who became a hero of the Vilna ghetto, blew up a German troop train in 1942 in the first successful major act of anti-Nazi sabotage.[6] Teenager Sulia Rubin escaped a ghetto in Belarus but was captured after joining the forest partisans; tortured for hours, she told the Germans nothing.[7] Lise Magun, too, was tortured to death without a word of betrayal, and *Lize Ruft*—"Lize Calls"—soon became the rallying cry of the ghetto fighters.[8] Niuta Teitelboim grew up in an ultra-

Defense volunteers in Israel, 1941. The middle poster
says, "Your place is here."
Taussig/Hulton Archive. Used by permission of Getty Images.

Orthodox family in Warsaw, but by chance she looked like an
Aryan beauty. "Little Wanda with the Braids," as she was
called, would charm her way past guards to German officers
and shoot them dead.[9] She, too, died by torture—there'd
been a huge reward for her capture—and after the war was
posthumously awarded Poland's highest combat medal.

These young women's stunning courage had its match in Israel. Sarah Aaronsohn, one of the earliest settlers, led a Jewish spy network to help the British in World War I. The Turks captured and tortured her, but she took her own life.[10] Devorah Drachler and Sarah Chizik were among ten legendary heroes who died in 1920 defending the northern outpost of Tel Hai. In the 1940s, *tens of thousands* of women served in the Haganah—the Jewish Defense Force—and made up a third of the Palmach, a famously daring commando force.

During Israel's War of Independence, women escorted convoys through embattled stretches of countryside and fought to defend settlements. Dr. Ruth Westheimer, the funny and wise American sex expert, was one of those fighters,[11] as was Shorika Braverman, a kibbutz member who had previously parachuted behind Nazi lines and joined the Yugoslav partisans.[12] She later ran the units training women soldiers in Israel. In subsequent wars women served on the front lines as radio operators and medics; one piloted a plane that parachuted infantry into combat.

Most unmarried Jewish women in Israel still serve for two years after high school. Many are expert shots who train men for combat. Some volunteer for work on the front lines or as pilots. Some teach tank crews, leading to occasional problems with their eighteen-year-old male-chauvinist trainees, but the trainees are routinely won over by the young women's professionalism and total command of the skills the men will need to survive.[13] These are the women who unmanned the puerile American fop Portnoy; they hark back to the time of Judges, when the first Israeli state was taking shape.

Oone judge, Deborah, was known for wisdom and prophecy, but even more for military leadership, as the Canaanite army discovered to its sorrow. After decisively defeating them, she sang her own praises:

> The open land was gone in Israel,
> Gone until Deborah arose,
> Arose a mother in Israel . . .
> Awake awake, O Deborah!
> Awake awake, let the song ring out![14]

But hers is not the only model of physical courage. During the same war, Jael clinched a victory by entertaining an enemy general: "Then Jael . . . took a tent pin and grasped the mallet. When he was fast asleep from exhaustion, she approached him stealthily and drove the pin through his temple until it went down to the ground."[15]

The apocryphal book of Judith tells of a wealthy young widow, "very lovely to behold. Her husband had left her gold and silver, men and women slaves, livestock, and field. . . . No one spoke ill of her, for she feared God with great devotion."[16] But her people, overrun by a vast Assyrian army, had lost heart. She "took off her widow's garments, bathed her body with water, and anointed herself with precious ointment. She combed her hair, put on a tiara, and dressed herself. . . . She put sandals on her feet, and put on her anklets, bracelets, rings, earrings, and all her other jewelry. Thus she made herself very beautiful, to entice the eyes of all the men who might see her."[17] So arrayed, Judith crosses enemy lines to see the enemy general Holofernes, agreeing to spy for him and be his concubine. But on the night when he intends to take up her offer, he drinks himself into a stupor and Judith beheads him with his own sword—also a turning point in *that* war. If Deborah is the forerunner of Israel's fighting women, Jael and Judith are the models for women like Niuta Teitelboim—"Little Wanda with the Braids"—and the Mossad spies who defend their country by means of seduction.

But one of the great Jewish tales of a woman who "becomes" a man has nothing to do with war or violence but rather another kind of contest embedded in Jewish life for millennia. This is I. B. Singer's *Yentl the Yeshiva Boy*, which gazes long and hard on a secret male world through a young woman's eyes. Yentl—played by Barbra Streisand in the film version—is a girl with a natural gift for study, and her gentle father, feeling ambivalent, teaches her. " 'Yentl,' " he says, " 'you have the soul of a man.' 'So why was I born a woman?' 'Even heaven makes mistakes.' " When he dies prematurely she cannot face the life she is destined for—serving some unknown man far less bright than she is—so "Yentl cut off her braids, arranged sidelocks at her temples, and dressed herself in her father's clothes." She joins the others making their way from countless small towns to the yeshiva.

There Avigdor, her best friend, study partner, roommate, and eventual object of her affections, helps and protects her. A secret in *his* past prevents him from marrying his beloved, Hadass, so he arranges for Yentl—now Anshel—to marry her. She somehow deflowers naive Hadass, who by now is in love with the changeling. Yentl finally shows herself to Avigdor (literally—the only way to make him believe her), and after his initial shock (they have broken half the commandments regarding men's relations with women) they are tempted to marry each other. But Yentl says, " 'I wanted to study the Gemara and Commentaries with you, not darn your socks!' " She divorces Hadass, who marries Avigdor after all, and they name their first child, a son, Anshel.

First published in 1962, *Yentl* may have helped open Jewish male bastions to women. Second-wave feminism made many women aspire to be rabbis, cantors, and lay synagogue leaders, to study and write Jewish law, commentary, and theology, even Orthodox theology. Now the Jewish world is full of these marvelous "changelings," who are comfortable both in their female bodies and their Jewish professional roles.

17

Jewish Genes?

This book began as an essay on the Jewish body, but from the first sentence we had to consider the Jewish mind. The people who circumcised the penis to perfect it, to complete God's creation-work on their bodies, also reimagined God as bodiless and spread this odd idea to billions of people throughout the world. If the Jewish body with its clipped foreskin, its monthly bloody show, its swine- and shrimp-free gut, its mandated yet spiritual copulations, its ritual cleansing in the sacred bath, and its rapid maggoty degeneration after death was one obsessive focus of Jewish law, even this was trumped by the Jewish obsession with mind.

If the Jews ever came close to worshipping anything other than God, it was text—God's word as revealed in the Torah. And after the destruction of their First Temple and their exile in Babylon, study and prayer supplanted animal sacrifice. Returning, rebuilding their Temple, again running streams of sacrificial animal blood down the Temple steps on festival days, they still read, studied, and argued Torah. And after that Temple, too, was destroyed, they literally clung to the Torah, taking it with them to every corner of the planet, kissing the scroll through its velvet cover, draping it with ornaments of silver, uncoiling it lovingly to chant from and bless, and living their moment-to-moment bodily lives by its teachings.

What does it mean? was a question always on their lips, and by this they meant not just the sense of the sentences, paragraphs, and chapters, but intent, say, of repeating the same word twice in close succession, the mathematical value of letters, or even the broadening or ornamentation of a letter by careful calligraphers copying it again and again for centuries. Because of course it was God's own intent that they were pondering.

"*On the lips of God, in the hand of Moses*" goes the passage, sung to a haunting melody every Sabbath morning by Jews on every continent. This bodiless God has at least metaphoric lips, which dictated the Torah to the prophet's faithful hand. So even as the Temple stood, as lambs without blemish and almost without number had their throats cut by blades without flaws on the flawlessly sacred altar, the great debates that were to become the Talmud had begun. Ultimately this shelf of books, so misunderstood and condemned by the enemies of the Jews, recorded the arguments among the greatest Rabbis in each generation for centuries, and in the end was distilled into the laws Jews live by.

Thus reading, interpreting, pondering, arguing, and arguing about arguing in an endless meta-succession were of the essence of Jewishness almost from the beginning. *Answers a question with a question* is not just a joke but a way of life, a discipline of thought, an insistence on leaving no point of law or practice undebated, no narrative unfathomed, no symbol undeciphered, no intellectual stone—no page—unturned.

For the outsiders, whether enemies or not, Jewish body and Jewish mind have always been of a piece, because until recently in history no one doubted that ethnic groups had minds and hearts as biologically distinctive as their bodies. Aristotle's student called the Jews "philosophers by race." Greco-Roman anti-Semites and early Church fathers alike conflated the physical distinctiveness of Jews with alleged traits of character—greed, sloth, weakness, cowardice, and depravity. Literary greats from Chaucer to Dickens did the same, so by the late nineteenth century there was no question in the minds of most European intellectuals that the Jews were a race as immutable mentally as physically; from this in due course followed the murder of six million.

No longer. Today's intellectuals deny that the Jews are a race, or even a people, insisting that Judaism, like Christianity and Islam, is not tied to any particular ethnic group. For almost all it is the only respectable opinion. The greatest tragedy in Jewish, perhaps in all history, was the result in part of an insistence on Jewish *people*hood—ethnicity, blood, genes, race. Surely the memory of the Shoah should suppress, for all future time, any notion of Jewish biological difference? Unfortunately, for simplicity and political correctness, or even perhaps for the ultimate physical safety of the Jews, the question of Jewish peoplehood cannot be answered through philosophy or politics. The Nazis got it wrong, but that does not mean that the most opposite answer we can conceive of must therefore be right. So how do we answer it?

Anthropologists today think about race in ways that are completely different from those of fifty years ago, when we already thought we had absorbed the lessons of the devastating racial theories of the early twentieth century. What social and cultural anthropologists mean by it has little to do with biology. They see, quite accurately, a unified species of six billion human hearts and minds artificially carved up by invidious distinctions—almost always visible ones, like skin color or the shapes of eyes or noses. This tendency reflects the human weakness for dichotomizing the world. Night and day, pure and polluted, right and wrong, and of course black and white—each pair of contrasting opposites turns a natural continuum into a false dichotomy.

Each pairing also assigns values; one is better than the other. When we split the human world into races, only one division matters: *we* and *they*, *us* and *them*. The underlying reality is statistical, human differences a continuum, but the dichotomizing urge leads us again and again to *we* and *they*. And of course, *we* are better. The psychoanalyst Erik Erikson called it pseudospeciation, a way of excluding certain people from the species itself, literally dehumanizing the other. Of all who have been most hurt by pseudospeciation, Jews rank very high, probably first on the list. One would think that fact alone would make us leave the subject of biological differences alone.

Until *very* recently, even in a book about the Jewish body, we might have ignored the question that the enemies of the Jews thought they had the answer to: *Is there—truly—anything genetically distinctive about the Jews?* In the long-past days of ten or twenty years ago, you could point to the enormous physical variety of Jews in different parts of the world. You could highlight the fact that conversion to Judaism is perfectly possible and that therefore being Jewish is just like being Christian or Muslim—namely, allegiance to and faith in a religion that you can take or leave and that therefore has nothing to do with anything biological or hereditary.

I recall as a young man arguing with my father-in-law, no racist, but a sensible and liberal man, who had very tentatively suggested—even then, it was politically incorrect—that there might, just might, be something genetic about the great success of the Jews. I was thoroughly and haughtily convinced that there was not.

The trouble with this answer today is that we are in the genomic era. The Jewish genes, whatever they are, are not just part of the Jewish body, they are its wellspring. Emma Lazarus and Max Nordau were right to think that the Jewish body could be changed by force of will, and so it was, but there are limits. We cannot wave away the genes in a world where the human genome has been sequenced, the origins and variety of human genes are under vigorous study, and every day brings news about the relationship between specific genes and traits, both normal and abnormal. There is still no simple positive answer to the question *Are there Jewish genes?* but there is also no simple negative one, such as the one so many of us have relied on for so long. We will consider current ways of answering it, but first: *Who is a Jew?*

According to halakhah, Rabbinic law, a Jew is someone who had a Jewish mother, or who has converted according to Jewish law. For the Orthodox, including the Orthodox-controlled Interior Ministry of Israel (they decide who receives immediate citizenship under the Law of Return), the conversion must be by an Orthodox rabbi. For Conservative Jews, a Jew is someone born of a Jewish mother or converted by any ordained rabbi. And for Reform Jews, having a non-Jewish mother but a Jewish father is also now considered enough to make someone Jewish if he or she so chooses; they accept patrilineal as well as matrilineal descent.

As we will see, these varied definitions, but especially the traditional halakhic one, have strong implications for our question about the genes. But there are many other, less formal definitions of who is a Jew:

- A Jew is someone who believes in the Jewish God and tries to follow the laws derived from the Torah and the Talmud.
- A Jew is someone whose parents or grandparents believed those things.
- A Jew is someone who identifies with the history and traditions of the Jewish people.
- A Jew is someone who has Jewish children. (Former Israeli prime minister Shimon Peres, after he reached a certain stage in life, half-jokingly amended this to

"... who has Jewish grandchildren." Given the challenges to Jewish continuity, either makes sense.)

- And, finally, more than half-jokingly, a Jew is someone who claims to be Jewish, since who would be foolish enough to make the claim if they were not?

These are all cultural definitions, but (because conversion is not easy) the halakhic definition is largely a genetic one. It might be said that if only genes mattered, patrilineal descent would be accepted on a par with having a Jewish mother, but this is not the case. It's a wise child who knows its own father, and on average the relatedness of fathers to their purported children is a little less than that of mothers. This is not trivial; the switch from paternal to maternal descent in ancient times may have been due to rapes of Jewish women during Israel's wars.

None of these definitions is new, and all have been in use since Jews and Judaism began. One clue comes not from genetics but from archaeology: The people came first. This is true even if "Judaism" is not Rabbinic Judaism but the Temple religion. Call them Israelites, Hebrews, or what you will, they existed long before that Temple did, and before the laws of the Temple religion were set forth. In fact, the Israelites continuously occupied the places that are now part of Israel or Palestine throughout the time that, according to the Bible, they were sojourning and then enslaved in Egypt.

Some of them did sojourn there, and some of them were certainly carried off into slavery by Egyptian armies. But the bulk of them stayed put, and archaeologists find a remarkable continuity between that Israelite culture and the one that would characterize the Israelite kingdom—in other words, they gradually developed Jewish culture while most of them were living in the land that is now Israel. There were wars, but there is no evidence outside the Bible of a large-scale conquest of the land by an outside force that came from beyond the Jordan River. This is important, because if the Jews, or at least the Israelites, were a people before there was anything that could be called a Jewish religion, then what some Jews call "peoplehood" has priority.

Why all this history? Because, to anticipate our discussion of the genes, the latest evidence places the ancestors of today's Jews in that place and time.

Physicians and geneticists—and not just those who were enemies of the Jews—have long suspected that there might be something genetically different about this people. It was not easy for them, and it is not easy for me, to entertain this proposition in the wake of some six million murders of Jews supported by Nazi racial theory. But some facts at least were staring us in the face. Richard Goodman, an Israeli pediatrician, spent his life caring for and studying children with genetic diseases, and his major work, *Genetic Disorders Among the Jewish People*, published in 1979, described what was then known about these often-tragic ailments.[1]

Most of what Goodman taught us remains true, but we know much more.[2] At least forty genetic disorders either are confined to or are much more likely to occur in Jews than in others. This includes some diseases that other groups of people also get, but which Jews get through one or more mutations that are more or less specific to Jews. There is nothing unusual about this; people of African descent are almost the only ones who get sickle-cell anemia, while people of European descent (Jewish or not) are the most likely by far to get cystic fibrosis. Ethnic groups have not been pure, but they have mated among themselves more than with others; this inevitably makes some genes more common.

We now know exactly what the defect is for most "Jewish" single-gene diseases and the chemical path from gene to disease for many. But we have also confirmed some long-known facts. For example, not only are some genetic disorders more likely among Jews than non-Jews but culturally and geographically distinct groups of Jews also have some different diseases.

For example, Tay-Sachs disease is a devastating form of mental retardation found predominantly among Ashkenazic Jews. It is one of several "lysosomal storage diseases" characteristic of Ashkenazic Jews, a technical point that may be important. Normal brain cells grow extensions called dendrites, treelike structures that branch widely as listening devices for signals from other cells. The slimmest dendritic branches are covered with spines, which provide a greatly increased surface for the incoming connections. The spines respond to experience, changing shape and increasing in number and density as we learn.

But in Tay-Sachs a mutation damages a crucial enzyme ("hex A") that normally removes a toxic substance. Without it, the toxin builds to poisonous levels, bloating the dendrites and stripping them of spines. This steadily degrades the ability of brain cells to communicate, causing muscular and mental retardation and sometimes psychiatric disorders. Its genetic pattern is recessive, which means you need a double dose of the gene to have the disease, usually because each of your parents carries a silent single dose. The child usually dies before age five, while parents and doctors look on helplessly.

In torsion dystonia, which strikes children seven to ten, intelligence is normal or even better than average, but involuntary, sustained, twisting muscle contractions cause contorted postures, beginning in the legs in one child, in the arms or neck of another, leading to worsening disability. One dose of the gene can cause this one, but not every child who carries it gets it. Still, it occurs in one out of every two thousand to six thousand Ashkenazic Jewish children. It can be treated but not cured, and at present the path from gene to disease is unknown. There are many others: Gaucher's disease, Bloom syndrome, Fanconi's anemia, and more.

Since both my parents were deaf, I know a bit about genetic deafness. The kind suffered by Ashkenazic Jews (four times as often as for others of European descent) is caused by a defect in a protein called "connexin 26," part of a channel in nerve cells in the inner ear, and deafness can be mild or profound. My mother was profoundly deaf (she had 5 percent hearing in one ear, none in the other, and her speech was difficult to understand), but her case was probably not genetic; her parents and much older siblings remembered that her deafness followed a heat stroke when she was about two years old and had already begun learning language.

My father had no hearing in one ear and 25 percent in the other, which meant he could hear a little with a hearing aid, but his younger brother was profoundly deaf. My dad had a story about his deafness—that it followed his rolling off the counter of his parents' dry-goods store in Brooklyn and injuring his head. But when I asked him another time to tell me the cause of Sol's deafness, he gave me the same story.

Most likely my father and uncle had connexin 26 deafness. As with Tay-Sachs, one in every twenty-five or so Ashkenazic Jews is a carrier; when my paternal grandparents met and married they may have rolled the dice. They had four children, two of whom were deaf; although two carriers will on average have one in four children affected, two out of four is comfortably within the probabilities. As far as we could find out, there were no other cases of deafness in their ancestors or their descendants.

Except, perhaps, for me. I have lost the hearing in my right ear prematurely, and my left ear is not what it used to be. It could be the ordinary hearing loss of aging, but I am only sixty-one. Perhaps my Jewish body should be tested for connexin 26. If I have the gene, it will be doubly satisfying to know that this is one of those shared by Jews and Palestinians; my Palestinian friends and I are not speaking metaphorically when we say that we are cousins.

But the genes that hit home most for me are the ones for susceptibility to breast cancer. I lost my wife to that disease, and my two daughters are at risk for it. There can be a genetic tendency for anything, but the genes play a classic, very large role in just 5 percent of breast cancers. Some of the other 95 percent are influenced by many genes, but others are probably not genetic. And a disease that strikes one in every eight or nine women is so common that many thousands of breast cancer patients will have a mother, grandmother, aunt, or sister who had the same disease, for nongenetic reasons.

A family with *many* cases is a different story. Such families were intensively studied in the 1980s and '90s, and most of them were Ashkenazic Jews. Two genes, BRCA1 and BRCA2 (for BReast CAncer, often pronounced "bracka"), explained the excess of cancer in these families. They are tumor-suppressor genes, and when they mutate they don't suppress cancer growth as they should. They also greatly increase ovarian cancer risk. They are under active study and could lead to insights that will help not just Jews but all women with these cancers.

So even ignoring persecution, being "chosen" isn't always good. But how does all this help with the who-is-a-Jew problem? My brother and I understood what it meant to grow up in a handicapped family, and we certainly saw being Jewish as another handicap, but now it turns out that the two might be connected. Whether we talk about Tay-Sachs or deafness, the geneticist's conclusion is the same: Ashkenazic Jews were *to some extent* a genetic isolate. The italics are essential. Worldwide, thallasemia genes are unexpectedly common in Italians and Southeast Asians, sickle-cell anemia genes in Africans, and cystic fibrosis genes in Europeans. Blood type frequencies differ among populations, as do countless other genes and proteins. These facts don't mean that the human population has been broken up into isolated segments, but we do tend to mate more with people like ourselves, and Ashkenazic Jews are no exception.

DNA technology traces history in the genes and confirms much, but not all, of what the Jews have thought about themselves. Almost all the world's Jews have in common a substantial genetic resemblance to non-Jews of the Middle East. That is, the Jews of Surinam, Morocco, Poland, England, India, Afghanistan, and Brooklyn are all related to Christians and Muslims whose families have never in many centuries left Lebanon.

So Jewish peoplehood is a reality, and it traces to an origin in roughly the time and place, if not the exact manner, that Jews have always believed in. In ancient times the people expanded by conversion, but in the last millennium much less so. Anyone can convert to Judaism, and Jews by Choice, as they are respectfully known, are 100 percent Jewish according to Jewish law. A woman who converts renders her future daughters Jewish, and their daughters, and so on down the line, along with the sons of all those women. But it isn't easy to convert—anti-Semitism made it dangerous for Jews to accept converts, and the laws of the Sabbath, kosher food, menstrual purity, and, not least, circumcision were obstacles. Judaism, as liberal Jews insist, is neither a racial category nor a biological characteristic, yet the practice of Judaism has historically overlapped with a population that can, *to some extent*, be genetically defined.

But Jews also depart from this Semitic tendency in the direction of the surrounding peoples. They may think they have rarely or never intermarried, but Joseph, Moses, Ruth, Esther, and others in the Bible tell a different story, one underscored by the genes. Why do Moroccan Jews tend to look Moroccan, Indian Jews Indian, and Polish Jews Polish? There can only be one reason. We can assume, if we like, that proper conversion was involved—conversions of prospective spouses, or just of interested others. But we know genes were imported and therefore people must have been.

Then why these Ashkenazic genetic diseases? Two explanations are possible. First, the non-Jewish genes apparently came in close to the founding of the Ashkenazic population. Mitochondrial DNA, which is passed down only from mothers to daughters, suggests that all Ashkenazic women alive today are descended from a small number of women, perhaps as few as six. But these founding mothers may not have been born Jewish. Most likely the Jews who first came to Northern Europe were long-distance traders—very unlikely to have been women—who may have taken wives from the surrounding populations. There may have been kosher conversions, but rabbis must have been scarce. Perhaps, like Ruth, they simply declared that they would join the Jewish people and worship the God of Israel. After these founding events, though, very few women seem to have come in. In such a small founding population, some disease genes may concentrate by chance—what geneticists call a "founder effect"—and then be preserved by relative isolation.

The second explanation is new and far more controversial. A geneticist friend of mine and two of his colleagues (none of whom is Jewish) have published a theory in the *Journal of Biosocial Science* that stirred considerable debate even before it was printed.[3] It argues that Ashkenazic genetic diseases are the result of natural selection in favor of the carriers—a "balanced polymorphism."

Let me explain. Sickle-cell anemia (named after its misshapen red blood cells) is a devastating blood disease found mainly in children of African descent. You need a double dose of the bad gene to have the disease—it's recessive—but there are far more cases than with most recessive diseases—cystic fibrosis, for example. The cases of cystic fibrosis can be largely explained by mutations, which numerically balance premature deaths, leaving the disease to percolate along at a very low level.

But mutation could not explain most of the sickle-cell cases, so scientists began to search for another cause. As with all recessive genes, there are many more carriers than there are double doses. If carriers, with a single dose, were for some reason better off than those completely "normal," they would keep the sickle-cell gene around at a higher level, and there would be more children with the double-dose disease. It turned out this was just what was going on: Carriers are especially resistant to malaria, one of Africa's greatest killers, so they kept the sickle gene around and that gene, in the occasional double dose, produced a devastating anemia.

The sickle-cell finding led to a search for similar processes in other genetic diseases; few were found.

Enter the new theory about *Jewish* genetic diseases. It proposes a balanced polymorphism for not one but several Ashkenazic genes, starting from four observations. First, Jewish genetic diseases are too common to be explained by mutation alone. Second, after the founding of the Ashkenazic population, gene exchange was fairly low. Third, Ashkenazic Jews consistently score higher than other ethnic groups, including other Jews, on IQ tests, although not on *spatial* intelligence. Fourth, unusual conditions may have selected Ashkenazic Jews for higher intelligence. Except for the last, these claims are not controversial.

The researchers go on to argue that the defects in several of these diseases might be expected, in weaker form, to influence how brain cells grow. As they put it, the various defects fall on only a few pages of a standard biochemistry textbook, an extremely unlikely outcome by chance alone. For example, Tay-Sachs and Gaucher's disease cause brain cells to accumulate fatty molecules called sphingolipids, causing mental retardation. But at lower doses such as carriers might have, the same molecules could promote the growth and branching of extensions that connect to other cells.

The BRCA genes would fall on a different page of the chemistry book. They normally suppress cancer by repairing broken strands of DNA, but when they are defective, cancer cells multiply. However, they are also found in brain cells; they may cause cancer later in life but also could perhaps allow brain cells to multiply before birth, which might outweigh the disadvantage of breast cancer, which tends to occur after the genes are passed on. In fact, a study published in *Science*, America's leading science journal, in May 2008, confirmed that BRCA1 is part of a gene network that regulates the way nerve cells make extensions toward each other in order to connect.[4] A similar argument might be possible regarding some other Ashkenazic gene defects. Finally, it is known that torsion dystonia and an Ashkenazic disease of the adrenal gland (congenital adrenal hyperplasia) are both associated with higher IQ even in those affected, although it is not known why.

At this stage the theory has to be viewed as merely an intriguing hypothesis, but it cannot be dismissed out of hand. Ashkenazic Jews may have come under strong selection for intelligence, especially of the verbal and analytical kind. The researchers reason that restrictions on occupational choice in Christian Europe forced Jews into mercantile occupations. (As Theodor Herzl said, "We cling to money because onto money we were flung."[5]) These occupations would have demanded greater intelligence and would likely have resulted in more surviving children. However, we know that more Ashkenazic Jews throughout their history were involved in other occupations, including crafts, medicine, teaching, and scholarship.

Religious Jews have a system of education that created a tradition steeped in learning, but it may have done more. For centuries, the brightest young men from every village were sent to larger villages and then to towns and cities where there were centers of Torah learning. These young men competed for recognition and advancement under the withering, critical gaze of their masters. They boarded with families in these towns who were well-off enough to add a young male mouth to the table. And the very best scholars were often married off to the daughters of the town's wealthiest merchants. Others married rabbis' daughters, and some of the merchants' children were paired off among themselves. In either case these were the most intelligent young men, and their children were raised in the most comfortable environments.

Natural history is helpful here. Some species have a breeding ground in which males compete for females, who choose the best among them. Sometimes the males fight, as in the head-butting contests of antelope or bison. Sometimes they compete only in attractiveness; the dazzling beauty of the male peacock's tail results from countless generations of peahens more dazzled by one tail than another. Some theories of the rapid evolution of the human brain suggest that a similar process allowed our female ancestors to apply sexual selection to brain size. Maybe the guy who talked the best line, say, or who made the best stone tools, got the gal.

It is not beyond the realm of possibility that Rabbinical academies functioned in something like this way. If so, it is not surprising that the Ashkenazic Jews excel in verbal and analytical intelligence, the skills that were prized in the academies. It is also not surprising that they are weak in spatial skills, which were not. Add to this hypothetical process the founder effect and moderate inbreeding and you might have a recipe for concentrating intelligence. It may also help explain why, even after the murder of six million, people of Ashkenazic descent make up 80 percent of the world's Jews.

The genes are an invisible galaxy of molecular spirals, creating our bodies and then winding their way into every crevice of them. Could these minuscule bits of the body be in part responsible for the success of the Jewish mind? We don't yet know, but at the rate the science of genetics is advancing, we may soon find out.

EPILOGUE

W e have come full circle, tying certain inborn features of the Jewish body to the seemingly (in some way) special Jewish mind. In the beginning, the Jews were a people who came to believe in a God without a body. People had bodies, God did not. This revolutionary declaration of faith was a challenge thrown in the face of every cult and culture in the ancient world. Others, too, cherished their beliefs, prostrated themselves in tears at the feet of their gods and goddesses and danced around them in joy, begged them for triumph in war and fertility in barrenness, and thanked them with all their hearts for their children's lives and a few years of peace. They did not, of course, think that these figures, which they molded, chiseled, and carved themselves, *were* the deities, but they loved the representations almost as much as the gods and goddesses.

To all these people the Hebrews said: *You are charlatans and fools.* The ancient Greeks called them atheists, no doubt a general appraisal from the moment they began to try to purge the world of any but this one vast, abstract, invisible deity. Contempt? Resentment? Fear? These words perhaps begin to describe the feelings the Jews must have evoked in others, and they were mutual. The arrogance with which this tiny people declared the rest of the world's most cherished beliefs to be wrong is stunning in retrospect. And the idea of a god without a body, although now embraced by billions, remains hard to grasp.

The Jews became the people of the book, "a race of philosophers" who conversed about God, but also conversed about their own human bodies, and wrote about them—so much so that two millennia later a Jewish scholar would call them "the people of the body," although more precise perhaps would be "the people of the Book about the body." They could not take the body for granted. It and what was put into it had to be frequently purified and blessed. Even what came out of it was worth a blessing, praise for the God who had made this marvelous machine, and in his own image—although what that meant exactly led to thirty centuries of heated discussion. Ironically, this endless talk about God and God's word may have created conditions that changed the brain, the bodily basis of the mind.

They wanted to keep the body pure but not to deprive it of pleasures, even messy ones. Self-abnegation was largely forbidden, but woe to him who took pleasure randomly, injuring or insulting man, woman, or God. Guidelines for pleasure were as important as pleasure itself. The Jewish body was a temple, not to be defiled by either deprivation or excess. But at death it soon became an abomination, something useless, and had to return to its origin in dust. Yet this was not a denigration—quite the opposite; once the machine stopped working, according to God's will, stopped housing the apparatus of the human mind and soul, it was worthless, an insult to the magnificent vessel it had lately been.

This reverence for the body led Jews to the art of medicine—anatomical curiosity raised to a magnificent obsession, and the result was the ultimate mitzvah: Perfect and repair the unfinished work of God. Whether ancient Rabbis groping for truths about health, medieval physicians with the Torah on one hand and the works of Galen on the other, ministering to the very real ailments of their patients, or secular Nobel laureates of Jewish heritage discovering new things about the body, some of the brightest Jews were always drawn to the side of those—Jewish or not—who were physically suffering.

But they never believed there was any suffering like their own, and in the end perhaps they were right. Their God had chosen them for greatness and misery in one stroke—and then, again and again. Chosen-ness for the Jews has meant enslavement in Egypt and Babylonia, destruction of their homeland and sacred Temple twice, near genocide by the Romans, centuries of incitement by the Catholic Church, banishment from countless communities, confinement in ghettos, mass expulsion from Spain, centuries of savage "Inquisition" and pogroms, and, finally, after a few generations of "emancipation," the biggest and best-organized mass murder in history. The embodied Christian God was tortured and killed, but the Jewish body has been mortified millions of times over. So has the metaphoric body of the Jewish people.

It is little wonder that self-defense became an obsession with the Jews, and that modern Israel is a rallying point for every Jew who understands the past. Israelis are the ultimate muscle-Jews, and they are also automatic-rifle-Jews, tank-Jews, fighter-jet-Jews, and, as a final answer to relentless persecution, nuclear-weapons-Jews. All this is an extension of a new Jewish body—or, really, a born-again one, since Joshua, Deborah, Samson, David, Judah Maccabee, Bar Kochba, and others displayed and deployed such force in ancient history and legend. Not all of this muscle-flexing has been either successful or good; some of it has led to Jewish tragedy and tears. But the Jews tried mental strength and physical weakness for eighteen centuries with results that can at best be described as mixed. They have now decided to try strength in both and have built a Jewish body that nearly matches the Jewish mind. It's worth a try.

How will the Jews relate to the body in the future? Will they continue to build muscle as an ethnic and national duty? Use cosmetic surgery more than others? Participate fully in the worldwide trend to obesity? Hate themselves for feeling soft? Fight and kill and die to ensure their survival as a people? What role will the body play in their ongoing, constantly changing concept of themselves? We cannot answer these questions definitively, but we can answer a different one: How many Jewish bodies will there be in the not-too-distant future? This one has plausible answers.

Jews have always been few in number and have found strength in weakness; this may be the key to their success. But today a question mark hangs over the Jewish demographic future. Israeli Jews are reproducing, but much more slowly than non-Jews within and around their country. American Jews are simply not replacing themselves. Numbers have dwindled in the past several censuses, despite substantial emigration from the former Soviet bloc countries and Israel. For every hundred Jewish deaths there are eighty-five births, and Jewish women exceed their non-Jewish counterparts in childlessness at every age. Of Jews who marry, one in three marries a non-Jew, and most mixed couples do not raise Jewish children. American Jews are in violation of what philosopher Emil Fackenheim has put forward as the 614th commandment: *Do not grant Hitler a posthumous victory.*

There are many reasons for the demographic crisis. Jews are economically successful, educated, and egalitarian; this guarantees that the general trend toward smaller family size will affect them strongly. Jewish women have been feminist leaders and have justly embraced a spectrum of career tracks that were closed to them for centuries; these are not all easily compatible with the "mommy track." Then, too, the financial cost of raising a child into that ambitious upper-middle-class world has never been greater, and there are only so many hours in the day to drive kids from school to soccer practice to bat mitzvah lessons. But there are also anatomical reasons.

Perhaps the Jewish body—the American Jewish body at least—needs a new and different kind of revival. Israeli Jews have built up real and metaphoric muscle and American Jews, getting buff in the safety of pricey gyms, have done the same in their own much safer way. But despite the apparent allure of these high-toned bodies, they must in some sense be desexualized, because their owners are not reproducing in numbers consistent with a sound Jewish future.

Perhaps it's not hard to see why. Pregnancy isn't buff, and having your vulva stretched and nipples yanked by a tiny, whining body exuding foul-smelling excretions is not exactly the yuppie ideal. Even fatherhood cuts way into your treadmill time, and as for that stretched vulva . . . You get the point. Sex is great, but it's a mess, and its results are even more of a mess, not to mention a pain in the butt and other organs. The Rabbis embraced the mess and the pleasure alike; all right, they were men, but so did ordinary Jewish men and women for millennia.

Perhaps now the Jewish body needs to become less narcissistic and more open to the reproductive mess, and the Jewish body politic needs a pronatalist program. Births could be subsidized, including births to unmarried Jewish women, and infertility programs need communal support. Child care and preschool programs should be greatly expanded and free. And sex—yes, sex—should be vigorously promoted. This can be perfectly kosher and according to Jewish law. According to Rabbi Chizkiya, the medieval sage, when you get to heaven God will demand to know why you didn't indulge more in the pleasures that were permitted.

The Rabbis promoted sex between husband and wife as the key to the Jewish future and a balm for the marital bond. But the separation of sex and reproduction has reached unprecedented levels. The Rabbis went unprotected sex one better by forbidding sex for twelve infertile days a month— so pent-up lust would prime the demographic engine. Perhaps more Jewish couples could follow this Orthodox plan, but there may be more secular ways to accomplish the same thing. A birth-control buyback program for monogamous married couples? A serious money prize for the third, and more for the fourth, fifth, and sixth babies? Free Viagra? Jews should consider whatever it takes to put more Jewish bodies on the planet, not to outreproduce anyone else, just to replace the enormous attrition. Jewish numbers today are barely where they were before the Holocaust, and they are not growing.

Biblical stories, the Song of Songs, and the Talmud present sexuality as a normal, healthy ideal. Modern Jewish writers have made it a central theme in all its messy absurdity, brutal humor, inescapable pressure, more-than-occasional tenderness, and transcendent beauty. The organ God commanded Abraham to perfect—in exchange for enormous fertility—and its womanly counterpart have been objects of puzzlement and reverence for Jews from ancient times. As they understood, these parts of the body are meant to get together, in proper ways, but early and often, and with minimal obstacles between them and the Jewish bodies of the future. They broke the glass and got going. Abraham's descendants may be as numerous as the stars, at least the ones that he could see, but some of the stars are going out. To replace them, Jewish bodies simply have to do what *any* bodies do—what comes naturally.

The Bible relates the ancestral and religious story of Jews proud of their faith, but also of their bodies. Abraham is a warrior, in a time when you fought not with machines but with your body, and his wife, Sarah, has dangerous beauty. Jacob wrestles with an angel or perhaps even with God, and wins, and he makes no secret of his disappointment when he has to marry Leah before he can marry the prettier Rachel. David slays his ten thousands and Bathsheba's beauty tempts him to adultery and worse, yet her son by him becomes the wise, strong, handsome Solomon, who himself beds a thousand wives and concubines.

Yet the stories also reveal the body's limits and threats. Esau, the ruddy, healthy hunter, the elder twin and his father's favorite, is tricked and cast aside by his mother and brother, placing intelligence and faith over might and even legal right; famished, he trades his birthright for porridge, and his brother apes his superior body with a goatskin. Samson is supernaturally strong, but his penchant for highly desirable non-Jews and breaking his vows to God lead him to lose his strength and die blind in a triumphant but tragic catastrophe. David may be a warrior-hero, but his first claim to fame is that, as a lyre-strumming shepherd boy, his faith, not his strength, allows him to beat a lion and an ominous warrior-giant.

Still, you could say that the ancient Hebrews, including the greatest heroes of the Bible, had a respect for physical prowess almost rivaling that of the Greeks. It is not for nothing that (except for a dearth of gods) parts of the books of Judges, Samuel, Chronicles, and Kings sound like the *Iliad*. Monotheistic or pagan, Bronze Age virtue entailed an utterly physical warrior prowess.

But after the destruction of even the First Temple, in

tears by the rivers of Babylon, the Hebrews—now Jews—lost faith not in God, but in physical strength and structures. They harked back to the "strong hand and outstretched arm" with which their Lord God brought them out of the Land of Israel; and, ironically, the strength of this officially unembodied God, this metaphoric arm and hand, would be what they increasingly relied on.

Although they got Jerusalem back and built their Second Temple, a degree of skepticism prevailed toward everything physical. Animal sacrifice resumed, but Torah study grew alongside it; texts, abstractions, interpretations became more important than ever. True, there was some Jewish power, but in the shadow of Persian, then Greek, then Roman power. The Greco-Roman physical ideal tempted many Jews, and in the end some drifted away, reversing their centuries of Jewish faith and covenant even as they reversed their circumcisions.

But these were only the lost ones; the main stream of Jewish history now flowed in new paths. While much of Europe pursued the Apollonian ideal of athletic prowess and physical beauty, Jewish bodies bent over books. By the end of this phase of Jewish history, it was the life of the mind, not that of body, that produced the greatest heroes. And so it largely remained for eighteen centuries, until the increasingly untenable conjunction of mental power with physical weakness pointed to the end of the Jewish faith and people. This was when women and men like Emma Lazarus, Max Nordau, and Theodor Herzl called the Jewish people back to the life of the body, and saved them.

Or rather, with their inspiration, Jews saved themselves. Thousands of women and men, mostly young and strong, left the homes their ancestors had lived in for centuries—in Russia, Poland, Germany, France, England, Turkey, Egypt, and elsewhere—for the home their ancestors had lived in even before that. They would become a people of the Land—a people such as Jews had once upon a time been, before the long and vast hiatus of exile—which they would work and defend with their bodies; to paraphrase Nehemiah and Emma Lazarus, with a trowel in one hand and a rifle in the other.

They did this, and they revived the body of the Jewish people. But after centuries in which Jews were hated because they were weak (and treated accordingly), they are hated today because they are strong. Strong is better. Or as Golda Meir put it, "If we have to have a choice between being dead and pitied, and being alive with a bad image, we'd rather be alive and have the bad image." At this writing Meir's forced choice is as relevant as ever. The Nobel prizes, university presidencies, and commercial fortunes keep coming, but now these achievements of the mind are accompanied by a new idea of the Jewish body, one that has earned the Jews a new kind of respect in the world, and one that will likely persist for some time.

G olda Meir, prime minister of Israel from 1969 to 1974, occasionally tried to explain her motivation. As a child in Russia in the first few years of the twentieth century, she had witnessed terrifying anti-Semitic violence. In one pogrom she was playing with her friends in the street, and Cossacks spurred their horses to jump over the children's heads. The impression on her child's mind was indelible. "If there is any logical explanation for the direction that my life has taken," she once said, "it is the desire and determination to save Jewish children from a similar scene and from a similar experience."[1]

Now consider: forty years *after* what the child Golda witnessed, one and a half million children were murdered by the Germans and their Ukrainian, Lithuanian, Polish, French, and other collaborators. To try to grasp this number, think of an American elementary school, which on average will have about five hundred children in it, and do the math. We are talking about more than three thousand elementary schools full of children, seized, often tortured, and murdered—thrown out of windows, heads smashed on walls, slowly murdered by experiment, starvation, typhus, and of course the standard quicker methods of shooting, gassing, and cremation. If Meir was motivated by the pogroms she saw as a child in Russia, what motivation must the seventh million have had after seeing the almost quaint anti-Semitic terror she experienced multiplied millions of times? What must the average Israeli high school student think after really absorbing these facts?

So the Zionist legacy of the new Jewish body became infused with mournful laments and a heady mixture of hope, determination, and, yes, rage that emerged from the ashes of millions of Jewish corpses. The body shaped by these experiences and infused with these emotions is quite properly dangerous. When Israelis say "never again" they mean something very serious. They don't mean never again except if they have to fight and die fighting, or never again if, inadvertently, some innocents have to die, or never again except if they have to make nuclear weapons, or never again except if they have to build a wall to protect their children. No nation so threatened would tolerate exceptions to its security, least of all one fresh with the wounds of history's most horrific mass murder. As long as there are Jewish bodies with mouths to say it and hands to raise in their own defense, they just mean *never again.*

FOR FURTHER READING

Because of the ever-present suspicion of special pleading, I like to recommend books and articles by non-Jews. For general background, read Paul Johnson's magisterial *A History of the Jews* (New York: Harper & Row, 1987). For the contributions of the Jews to civilization ancient and modern, read Mark Twain's *Concerning the Jews* (Philadelphia: Running Press, 1985), Thomas Cahill's *The Gifts of the Jews* (New York: Random House, 1999), and Charles Murray's "Jewish Genius," published in *Commentary* in April 2007. For the history of Jewish persecution, read Father Edward Flannery's *The Anguish of the Jews* (New York: Macmillan, 1965) and James Carroll's *Constantine's Sword* (Boston: Houghton Mifflin, 2001). For a sweeping history of Zionism, read Conor Cruise O'Brien's *The Siege* (New York: Simon & Schuster, 1986).

For deeper and more detailed accounts of the Jewish body, two (Jewish) scholars are indispensable. Culture historian Sander Gilman's many books touching on this subject include *The Jew's Body* (New York: Routledge, 1991), *Making the Body Beautiful* (Princeton, N.J.: Princeton University Press, 1999), *Jewish Frontiers* (New York: Palgrave Macmillan, 2003), and *Fat Boys* (Lincoln: University of Nebraska Press, 2004). For an anthropological perspective, the essential works are by Howard Eilberg-Schwartz, including *The Savage in Judaism* (Bloomington: Indiana University Press, 1990) and his edited collection, *People of the Body* (Albany: State University of New York Press, 1992). For the religious Jewish outlook on sexuality and women's bodies, I recommend *Rereading the Rabbis: A Woman's Voice*, by Judith Hauptman (Boulder, Colo.: Westview Press, 1998), and *Marital Intimacy*, by Rabbi Avraham Peretz Friedman (Linden, N.J.: Compass Books, 2005).

Even after an Orthodox upbringing, I have learned much from Harvey E. Goldberg's *Jewish Passages: Cycles of Jewish Life* (Berkeley: University of California Press, 2003), the most useful basic *secular* work on the anthropology, history, and symbolism of Jewish rites of passage through the life cycle, from birth to death. The German Propaganda Archive—http://www.calvin.edu/academic/cas/gpa/—created by Randall Bytwerk, is an indispensable guide to a chilling and disturbing subject. Finally, I have long been inspired by the images in Yigal Lossin's *Pillar of Fire: The Rebirth of Israel: A Visual History* (Jerusalem: Shikmona Publishing, 1983; Yoram Sabo, photo researcher) and the accompanying television series from the Israel Broadcasting Authority.

NOTES

Preface

1. Howard Eilberg-Schwartz, "The Problem of the Body for the People of the Book," in *People of the Body: Jews and Judaism from an Embodied Perspective*, ed. Howard Eilberg-Schwartz, pp. 17–46 (Albany: State University of New York Press, 1992).

Prologue

1. For insightful renditions and interpretations of these stories, see Judith Hauptman, *Rereading the Rabbis: A Woman's Voice* (Boulder, Colo.: Westview Press, 1998); the quotes are on pp. 40–45.

2. "The Fruitful Cut"

1. The Bible translations in this chapter are from the King James Version, except where otherwise indicated. In general, throughout the book, for ease of comprehension and for accuracy, I have tried to use the Jewish Publication Society translation, *JPS Hebrew-English Tanakh* (Philadelphia: Jewish Publication Society, 1999). Otherwise, as indicated, where it does not raise questions of accuracy, I have used the King James Version, which is far superior as literature. In my view, many of the departures from the KJV in the JPS translation are gratuitous—neutral in terms of meaning and clarity and pedestrian as English prose or poetry. (Compare the two translations of Psalm 23 to see what I mean.)

2. Rabbi Moshe Weissman, *The Midrash Says: The Book of Beraishis* (Brooklyn, NY: Bnai Yakov Publications, 1980), p. 153.

3. Howard Eilberg-Schwartz, *The Savage in Judaism: An Anthropology of Israelite Religion and Ancient Judaism* (Bloomington: Indiana University Press, 1990), chap. 6.

4. Harvey E. Goldberg, *Jewish Passages: Cycles of Jewish Life* (Berkeley: University of California Press, 2003), p. 28. Chapter 2 is excellent on the constancies and variations in the customs surrounding circumcision among Jewish cultures.

3. Greeks and Jews

1. Camille Paglia, *Sexual Personae: Art and Decadence from Nefertiti to Emily Dickinson* (New Haven, Conn.: Yale University Press, 1990), p. 72.

2. Shaye J. D. Cohen, *From the Maccabees to the Mishnah* (Philadelphia: Westminster Press, 1987), chap. 2; David Stern, "Hellenism and Hebraism Reconsidered," *Poetics Today* 19(1) (1998): 1 17.

3. D. Schultheiss, M. C. Truss, C. G. Stief, and U. Jonas. "Uncircumcision: A Historical Review of Preputial Restoration," *Plastic and Reconstructive Surgery* 101(7) (1998): 1990–98; Robert G. Hall, "Epispasm: Circumcision in Reverse," *Bible Review* (August 1992): 52–57.

4. The quotations are from William Arrowsmith's translation of *The Bacchae*, in *The Complete Greek Tragedies: Euripides Volume III*, ed. David Grene and Richmond Lattimore, pp. 343–424 (New York: The Modern Library/Random House, 1959). The quotations are from pages 364, 373, 375, and 391.

5. Camille Paglia, *Sexual Personae: Art and Decadence from Nefertiti to Emily Dickinson* (New Haven, Conn.: Yale University Press, 1990), pp. 96–98.

6. For an excellent general discussion of the glass-breaking custom, see Harvey E. Goldberg, *Jewish Passages: Cycles of Jewish Life* (Berkeley: University of California Press, 2003), pp. 147–160, and for the custom of the stained sheet, p. 134. Deuteronomy 22:17 alludes to the latter custom.

4. Adam's Rib?

1. *The Talmud: The Steinsaltz Edition, Volume V: Tractate Bava Metzia, Part V,* commentary by Adin Steinsaltz, English edition trans. and ed. Israel V. Berman (New York: Random House, 1992), pp. 119–20.

2. Rabbi Avraham Peretz Friedman, *Marital Intimacy: A Traditional Jewish Approach* (Linden, NJ: Compass Books), p. 66.

3. Ibid., p. 68.

4. Ibid., p. 66.

5. This story is not in the Talmud but is recounted in a medieval text called *The Alphabet of Ben Sira*, dating from the ninth to eleventh centuries, which may not have recorded the sage Ben Sira's interpretations. Lilith is related to a prebiblical Mesopotamian goddess. She is mentioned in the Talmud as a sexual demon and the stories about her uppity response to Adam's domination must long precede this particular text.

6. Fischel, Lachower, and Isaiah Tishby. *The Wisdom of the Zohar: An Anthology of Texts, Volume II.* Translated by David Goldstein. 3 vols. Vol. II. (London: Oxford University Press, 1989), p. 538.

7. Ibid., p. 539.

8. Joshua Trachtenberg, *Jewish Magic and Superstition: A Study in Folk Religion* (New York: Atheneum, 1977), p. 29.

5. Dangerous Bodies

1. Weissler, Chava. "*Mizvot* Built into the Body: *Tkhines* for *Niddah,* Pregnancy and Childbirth," in *People of the Body: Jews and Judaism from an Embodied Perspective,* ed. Howard Eilberg-Schwartz (Albany: State University of New York Press, 1992) pp. 101–115.

2. Lis Harris, *Holy Days: The World of a Hasidic Family* (New York: Summit Books, 1985), pp. 147–48.

3. Glückel of Hameln, *The Memoirs of Glückel of Hameln,* trans. Marvin Lowenthal (New York: Schocken Books, 1977), pp. 150–51.

4. Younger Jews, including some who consider themselves religious, are increasingly breaking this prohibition. This is not simply to fit in; ironically, some use it to trumpet their Jewishness, with Stars of David

or Hebrew words such as "chai" (life) or "Shomer Achi" (my brother's keeper). In perhaps an even greater irony, Britney Spears and other celebrities have gotten Hebrew tattoos. The Leviticus quote is from the *JPS Hebrew-English Tanakh*, *Second Edition* (Philadelphia: The Jewish Publication Society, 1999).

6. God's Beard

1. This and subsequent Bible quotations in this chapter are from the *JPS Hebrew-English Tanakh*, *Second Edition* (Philadelphia: The Jewish Publication Society, 1999).

2. Naomi Janowitz, "God's Body: Theological and Ritual Roles of *Shi'ur Komah*," in *People of the Body: Jews and Judaism from an Embodied Perspective*, ed. Howard Eilberg-Schwartz (Albany: State University of New York, 1992) pp. 183–201.

3. Ibid., p. 189.

4. Ibid., p. 190.

5. Gershom Scholem, *Kabbalah* (New York: Dorset Press, 1974), p. 153.

6. Rabbi Joseph Gikatilla, *Gates of Light: Sha'are Orah*, translated by Avi Weinstein (San Francisco: HarperCollins/Bronfman Library, 1994), p. 7.

7. Scholem, *Kabbalah*, p. 152.

8. Perle Epstein, *Kabbalah: The Way of the Jewish Mystic* (New York: Doubleday, 1978), p. 47.

9. Lawrence Fine, "Purifying the Body in the Name of the Soul: The Problem of the Body in Sixteenth-century Kabbalah," in *People of the Body*, pp. 117–42.

10. Gershom Scholem, ed., *Zohar: The Book of Splendor: Basic Readings from the Kabbalah* (New York: Schocken Books, 1949), pp. 63–64.

7. "Hath Not a Jew Eyes?"

1. Julian Bene, *Still Spitting: Changing the Way We Deal with the Jewish Image in the Classics* (Unpublished manuscript, 2008). Cited by permission.

2. B. Netanyahu, *The Origins of the Inquisition in Fifteenth-century Spain*, 2nd ed. (New York: New York Review of Books, 2001).

8. Race and Destiny

1. Robert N. Proctor, *Racial Hygiene: Medicine Under the Nazis* (Cambridge, Mass.: Harvard University Press, 1988). In addition to Proctor's account, see Michael Kater, *Doctors Under Hitler* (Chapel Hill: The University of North Carolina Press, 1989), and Robert Jay Lifton, *The Nazi Doctors: Medicalized Killing and the Psychology of Genocide* (New York: Basic Books, 1986 2000).

2. See Lucy S. Dawidowicz, *The War Against the Jews, 1933–1945* (New York: Holt, Rinehart and Winston, 1975), for discussion and references.

3. Ibid., p. 20.

4. Ibid., p. 95.

5. Ernst Hiemer, *Der Giftpilz* (Nuremberg: Stürmerverlag, 1938). The translation, by Randall Bytwerk, is in the German Propaganda Archive of Calvin College, available at www.calvin.edu/academic/cas/gpa/thumb.htm and is used by permission.

6. David Welsh, *Propaganda and the German Cinema, 1933–45*, revised edition (London: I. B. Tauris, 2001); Linda Schulte-Sasse, "The Jew as Other Under National Socialism: Veit Harlan's Jud Süss." *The German Quarterly* 61:1, 1988, pp. 22–49.

7. Scene-by-scene accounts of *The Eternal Jew*, with many stills from the film and accompanying narration in German and English, are available at The Holocaust History Project, http://www.holocaust-history.org/der-ewige-jude/stills.shtml, which is frequently under electronic attack by anti-Semitic hackers but which vows to stay online.

8. Raul Hilberg, *The Destruction of the European Jews* (New York: Franklin Watts, 1973), p. 625.

9. Loc. cit.

10. Ibid., p. 627.

11. Ibid., p. 614.

12. Ephraim Oshry, *Responsa from the Holocaust. Selected and translated by the author from Sh'eilos utshuvos mima'akim* (New York: Judaica Press, 1983), pp. 74–75.

13. Ibid., pp. 51–53.

14. Ibid., pp. 72–73.

15. Ibid., p. 195.

16. Ibid., p. 196.

17. Deborah Lipstadt, *Denying the Holocaust: The Growing Assault on Truth and Memory* (New York: The Free Press, 1993).

9. Surviving

1. This chapter draws on a recently published memoir by Tosia Szechter Schneider, *Someone Must Survive to Tell the World* (Montreal: Polish-Jewish Heritage Foundation of Canada, 2007). The summary and quotations are used with permission.

10. The Body Returns

1. *The Talmud: The Steinsaltz Edition, Volume V: Tractate Bava Metzia, Part V,* commentary by Adin Steinsaltz, English edition trans. and ed. Israel V. Berman (New York: Random House, 1992), p. 122.

2. Louis Finkelstein, *Akiba: Scholar, Saint and Martyr* (Northvale, N.J.: Jason Aronson, 1990), p. 269.

3. Emma Lazarus, "An Epistle to the Hebrews," in *Four Centuries of Jewish Women's Spirituality: A Sourcebook*, ed. E. M. Umansky and D. Ashton (Boston: Beacon Press, 1992) pp. 102–103.

4. I owe much of my understanding of Nordau's role as a critic of the Jewish body (as well as some other themes of this book) to Sander Gilman, through both his published writings and personal communication. See especially his *The Jew's Body* (New York: Routledge, 1991). He is not of course responsible for my interpretations or errors.

5. Max Nordau, *Zionistische Schriften*, 2nd ed. (Berlin, 1923), pp. 484–486 as cited by Shlomo Avineri, *The Making of Modern Zionism* (New York: Basic Books, 1981), p. 101.

6. This and the subsequent Nordau quotes are from Max Nordau, "Jewry of Muscle," in *The Jew in the Modern World: A Documentary His-*

tory, ed. Paul R. Mendes-Flohr and Jehuda Reinharz (New York: Oxford University Press, 1980) pp. 434–35.

7. Theodor Herzl, *The Diaries of Theodor Herzl*, ed. and trans. Marvin Lowenthal (New York: Grosset & Dunlap, 1962), p. 76.

8. Ibid., p. 224.

9. Ha-Shomer Ha-Zair, "Our World-View," in *The Jew in the Modern World*, ed. Paul R. Mendes-Flohr and Jehuda Reinharz (New York: Oxford University Press, 1980), pp. 453–55.

10. Melford E. Spiro, *Kibbutz: Venture in Utopia* (Cambridge: Harvard University Press, 1956).

11. Paula Rayman, *The Kibbutz Community and Nation Building* (Princeton, NJ: Princeton University Press, 1981), p. 53.

12. Ibid., p. 55.

13. Howard Blum, *The Brigade: An Epic Story of Vengeance, Salvation, and World War II* (New York: HarperCollins, 2001), p. 162.

14. Chuck Olin and Matthew Palm. "In Our Own Hands: The Hidden Story of the Jewish Brigade in World War II," ed. Chuck Olin (Chicago/San Francisco: Chuck Olin Associates/KQED, 1998).

15. Blum, *The Brigade*, p. 162.

16. Amia Lieblich, *Kibbutz Makom: Report from an Israeli Kibbutz* (New York: Pantheon Books, 1981).

17. Ibid., pp. 8–9.

11. Tough Jews

1. My introduction to the history of Jewish boxing came through Douglas Century's superb *Barney Ross* (New York: Nextbook/Schocken, 2006), from which the next few pages are mainly drawn. For additional background see Ken Blady's *Jewish Boxers Hall of Fame* (New York: Specialist Press International, 1988) and Allen Bodner's *When Boxing Was a Jewish Sport* (Wesport/CT: Greenwood/Praeger Trade, 1997).

2. The remainder of this chapter draws on Albert Fried, *The Rise and Fall of the Jewish Gangster in America* (New York: Holt, Rinehart and Winston, 1980), supplemented and corroborated by Robert A. Rockaway, *But He Was Good to His Mother: The Lives and Crimes of Jewish Gang-*

sters (Jerusalem/New York: Geffen Publishing, 2000), and Rich Cohen, *Tough Jews: Fathers, Sons, and Gangster Dreams* (New York: Vintage Books, 1999). Cohen also wrote a superb book on Jewish resistance in World War II, *The Avengers* (New York: Vintage Books, 2001).

3. Fried, work cited, p. 70.

4. Ibid., pp. 28–35.

5. Ibid., pp. 94ff.

6. Cohen, *Tough Jews*, p. 47.

7. Rockaway, work cited, Chapter 8.

12. The Trowel and the Sword

1. Charles E. Silberman, *A Certain People: American Jews and Their Lives Today* (New York: Summit Books, 1985), p. 202.

13. The Eye of the Beholder

1. Sander L. Gilman, *The Jew's Body* (New York: Routledge, 1991), pp. 38–59.

2. Quoted by Gilman, ibid., pp. 41–42.

3. Max Nordau, "Jewry of Muscle." In *The Jew in the Modern World: A Documentary History*, ed. Paul R. Mendes-Flohr and Jehuda Reinharz, (New York: Oxford University Press, 1980), pp. 434–435.

4. Gilman, *The Jew's Body*, p. 53.

5. Ibid., p. 174.

6. Ibid., p. 179.

7. Ibid., p. 183.

8. Ibid., pp. 184–185.

9. Ibid., p. 187.

10. Sharon Romm, *The Changing Face of Beauty* (St. Louis, MO.: Mosby Year Book, 1992), p. 174.

11. This and the two subsequent quotations are as quoted by Beth Preminger in "The 'Jewish Nose' and Plastic Surgery: Origins and Implications," *Journal of the American Medical Association* 286(17) (2001): 2161.

12. Quoted by Keren Engelberg, "Making the Cut," JewishJournal .com, 2005–01–21; http://www.jewishjournal.com/home/print.php? id=13552.

13. Ibid.

14. Jane Gross, "As Ethnic Pride Rises, Rhinoplasty Takes a Nose Dive," *The New York Times*, Jan. 3 1999.

15. Preminger, "The 'Jewish Nose,' " p. 2001.

16. Engelberg, "Making the Cut."

17. I. S. Whitaker, R. O. Karoo, G. Spyrou, and O. M. Fenton, "The Birth of Plastic Surgery: The Story of Nasal Reconstruction from the Edwin Smith Papyrus to the Twenty-first Century," *Plastic and Reconstructive Surgery* 120(1) (2007): 327–36.

14. Bodily Fictions

1. Sander L. Gilman, *Franz Kafka* (London: Reaktion Books, 2005), p. 30.

2. Franz Kafka, *The Complete Stories*, pp. 271–72.

3. Ibid., p. 257.

4. Ibid., p. 139.

5. Gilman, *Franz Kafka*, 30.

6. Kafka, *The Complete Stories*, pp. 271–72.

7. Ibid., p. 257.

8. Philip Roth, *The Breast* (New York: Holt, Rinehart and Winston, 1972), p. 12.

9. Ibid., pp. 3–4.

10. Ibid., p. 10.

11. Ibid., p. 15.

12. Kafka, *The Complete Stories*, p. 277.

13. Ibid., p. 277.

14. Roth, *The Breast*, pp. 26–27.

15. John Felstiner, *Paul Celan: Poet, Survivor, Jew* (New Haven, Conn.: Yale University Press, 1995), pp. 31–32.

16. Ibid., p. 331.

17. Ibid., p. 289.

18. Abraham Sutzkever, *Poetishe Verk, Band Eyns: Lider Un Poemes Fun Di Torn 1934–47* (Tel Aviv: Yovel, 1963), pp. 278–79. Author's translation.

19. Cynthia Ozick, *The Shawl* (New York: Alfred A. Knopf, 1989), p. 9.

20. Ibid., pp. 23–24.

21. Ibid., pp. 64–65.

22. Isaac Bashevis Singer, *The Collected Stories* (New York: Farrar, Strauss, and Giroux, 1982), p. 132.

23. Philip Roth, *Portnoy's Complaint* (New York: Vintage, 1994), p. 76.

24. Ibid., p. 134.

25. Ibid., p. 256.

26. Ibid., p. 124.

15. Jewish Power

1. Except where otherwise indicated, the Bible translations in this chapter are from *JPS Hebrew-English Tanakh* (Philadelphia: Jewish Publication Society, 1999).

2. The JPS translation of the first part of this passage illustrates one of that version's problems. It reads: "He shall let them go because of a greater might; indeed, because of a greater might he shall drive them from his land." In the Hebrew, the words translated as "because of a greater might" are in both places *b'yad chazakah*—literally, with or by a strong hand. Should we infer that the meaning here is symbolic, not literal? Then why translate *bizroah n'tuyah* as "with an outstretched arm" a few lines down? The inconsistency is strange. Add to that the fact that, because of its use in the Passover seder, the phrase *b'yad chazakah u'vizroah n'tuyah*—translated as "with a strong hand and an outstretched arm"—is familiar to many generations of Jews in Hebrew and several in English, and the JPS choice becomes thoroughly baffling.

3. For ease of comprehension, which is admittedly its strength for modern readers, the JPS version is used here and for the rest of the chapter, except for the first few words of this passage, *Adonay ish milchama*. JPS renders them as "The Lord, the Warrior," but there is no justification in the Hebrew for departing from the KJV rendering, "The

Lord is a man of war," familiar through the centuries. Again, a few lines down, the JPS has "At the blast of Your nostrils the waters piled up," so this can't be about avoiding anthropomorphism. Why not say, "man of war"?

16. Deborah's Daughters

1. Ran Aaronsohn, "Through the Eyes of a Settler's Wife: Letters from the *Moshava*." In *Pioneers and Homemakers*, ed. Deborah S. Bernstein (New York: State University of New York Press, 1992), pp. 34–5.

2. Shulamit Reinharz, "Manya Wilbushewitz-Shohat and the Winding Road to Sejera," in *Pioneers and Homemakers*, ed. Deborah S. Bernstein, 95–118 (New York: State University of New York Press, 1992), p. 100.

3. Deborah S. Bernstein and Musia Lipman, "Fragments of Life: From the Diaries of Two Young Women," in *Pioneers and Homemakers*, ed. Deborah S. Bernstein, 145–64 (New York: State University of New York Press, 1992), p. 149.

4. Ibid., pp. 161–62.

5. Hannah Senesh, *Her Life and Diary*, trans. Marta Cohn (New York: Schocken Books, 1972); Peter Hay, *Ordinary Heroes: Chana Szenes and the Dream of Zion* (New York: G.P. Putnam's Sons, 1986).

6. Rich Cohen, *The Avengers: A Jewish War Story* (New York: Alfred A. Knopf, 2000), p. 63.

7. Nechama Tec, *Defiance: The Bielski Partisans* (New York: Oxford University Press, 1993), p. 54.

8. Abraham H. Foxman, "The Resistance Movement in the Vilna Ghetto," in *They Fought Back*, ed. Yuri Suhl, 163–175 (New York: Paperback Library, 1967), p. 167.

9. Yuri Suhl, "Little Wanda with the Braids," in *They Fought Back*, ed. Yuri Suhl, 62–66 (New York: Paperback Library, Inc., 1967).

10. Ze'ev Schiff, *A History of the Israeli Army: 1874 to the Present* (New York: Macmillan, 1985), p. 110.

11. Dr. Ruth Westheimer, http://drruth.com/content/view/42/27/, June 2, 2008.

12. Louie Williams, *Israel Defense Forces: A People's Army* (Tel Aviv: Ministry of Defense Publishing House, 1989), p. 322.

13. Ibid., p. 355.

14. Judges 5:7, 5:12, author's translation.

15. Judges 4:21, *JPS Hebrew-English Tanakh*, 2nd ed. (Philadelphia: The Jewish Publication Society, 1999).

16. Judith 8:7–8, *The New Oxford Annotated Bible, with the Apocryphal/Deuterocanonical Books: New Revised Standard Edition*, ed. Bruce M. Metzger and Roland E. Murphy (New York: Oxford University Press, 1994), p. 29AP.

17. Judith 10:3–4, Ibid., p. 31AP.

17. Jewish Genes?

1. Richard M. Goodman, *Genetic Disorders Among the Jewish People* (Baltimore: Johns Hopkins University Press, 1979).

2. H. Ostrer, "A Genetic Profile of Contemporary Jewish Populations," *Nature Reviews Genetics* 2(11) (2001): 891–98; I. Kedar-Barnes and P. Rozen, "The Jewish People: Their Ethnic History, Genetic Disorders and Specific Cancer Susceptibility," *Familial Cancer* 3(3 4) (2004): 193–99.

3. G. Cochran, J. Hardy, and H. Harpending. "Natural History of Ashkenazi Intelligence," *Journal of Biosocial Science* 38(5) (2006): 659–93.

4. Kenneth D. Bromberg, Avi Ma'ayan, Susana R. Neves, and Ravi Iyengar. "Design Logic of a Cannabinoid Receptor Signaling Network That Triggers Neurite Outgrowth," *Science* 320 (2008): 903–909.

5. Theodor Herzl, *The Diaries of Theodor Herzl*, ed. and trans. Marvin Lowenthal (New York: Grosset & Dunlap, 1962) p. 9.

Epilogue

1. Golda Meir quoted in "Middle East: The War and the Woman," *Time*, September 19, 1969; http://www.time.com/time/magazine/printout/0,8816,901451,00 html.

ACKNOWLEDGMENTS

Although only I am responsible for whatever may be wrong with this book, I take pleasure in acknowledging *some* of those who have helped. I thank Jonathan Rosen, editor of the Jewish Encounters series, for suggesting that I write a book about the Jewish body. Although at first neither of us knew quite what it would be about, together we discovered a path and liked what we found; Jonathan was a wise and supportive critic throughout.

My friends Steve Berman, Dr. Shlomit Ritz Finkelstein, and Dr. Herbert and Hazel Karp have enhanced my understanding of all things Jewish. My distinguished Emory colleagues Professor David Blumenthal and Professor Deborah Lipstadt have shared their insights for decades, and Professor Sander Gilman, a leading authority on the cultural history of the Jewish body, has been generous with knowledge and encouragement. Professor Randall Bytwerk of Calvin College, the creator of The German Propaganda Archive on the web, made important suggestions and helped with research on key images.

A new and rewarding collaboration for me has been with Ed Colker, who designed and illustrated a limited edition of my versions of some Avraham Sutskever poems. This work, Ed's encouragement, and my brief but inspiring acquaintance with Sutzkever, helped shape the vision expressed in *The Jewish Body*.

I am not religious, yet rabbis have touched my life for six decades, especially the late Rabbi Bernard Berzon (Orthodox), Rabbi Arnold Goodman (Conservative), and Rabbi Herbert Friedman (Reform), who at different stages contributed greatly to my understanding of Judaism, Jewishness, and Israel.

I have learned much in and about Israel from Dr. Pazit and Michael Sela, Dr. Susan Lourenço and Lt. Col. (IDF Res.) Louis Williams, Rabbi Emanuel Feldman, Dr. Eli Regev, and Rabbi and Professor David Schaps, among many others.

Although I was raised in a modern Orthodox family and synagogue, the Wexner Heritage Foundation, cofounded by Leslie Wexner and the late Rabbi Herbert Friedman, gave me a supplemental education in Jewish studies a quarter century later through their marvelous two-year seminar program. I made many contacts there that have helped and inspired me since.

My assistant Kathy Mote is a good friend and always an indispensable aide in my life and work, but in the final stages of this book, her efforts redoubled and made timely publication possible. Adam Garel-Frantzen, a researcher at Getty Images, helped us find some important photographs, and Yoram Sabo, the photo researcher for *Pillar of Fire*, led us to the source of the stunning anonymous photo of survivors of the Khodorkov pogrom.

Dan Frank, senior editor at Schocken/Pantheon, was encouraging throughout and made important editorial suggestions. His assistant, Fran Bigman, and her successor, Hannah Oberman-Breindel, were both helpful and tolerant of my concerns. Brian Barth, who designed the jacket, was highly creative and open to my suggestions. Rahel Lerner prepared the well-conceived and thorough Chronology. My agent and long-time friend Elaine Markson and her staff played their supportive role.

Marjorie Shostak was my wife, ally, and friend for thirty years, until her death in 1996. She gave me the three children, now formed and grown, to whom this book is dedicated. Without these four, my understanding of not just the Jewish but also the human body and spirit would have been radically impoverished.

Four years ago I married again; Ann Cale Kruger became my new partner in life, and her blessed spirit has helped me to heal the wounds of years of illness and loss. I know that not everyone gets a second chance. I am very happy and very grateful.

CHRONOLOGY

---

c. 1900 BCE   Time of the patriarch Abraham, who, at the age of ninety, is commanded by God to circumcise himself and all the men of his household.

c. 1280 BCE   God brings the Israelites out of Egypt "with an outstretched arm."

c. mid-twelfth century BCE   In the time of the judges, Israel is ruled by a female judge, Deborah. During one of Deborah's wars, Jael seduces the enemy general and kills him, tipping the scales in Israel's favor.

c. mid- to late-twelfth century BCE   Samson, a man of spectacular strength, leads Israel against the Philistines; he is undone by Delilah, who strips him of his strength.

c. 1000 BCE   David, who as a young man defeats the giant Goliath, becomes king of Israel;

he is renowned as a fighter, lover, and poet.

586 BCE The Kingdom of Judah is defeated by the Babylonians and its leaders exiled to Babylon.

539 BCE Persian Emperor Cyrus the Great, having defeated the Babylonian Empire, allows exiled Jews to begin to return to the land of Israel and to rebuild the Temple.

c. 407 BCE Athenian playwright Euripides writes *The Bacchae*, about the cult of the Greek God Dionysus.

322 BCE Alexander the Great conquers the land of Israel, spreading Hellenistic culture and its worship of the body.

174 BCE Jason, a Hellenizing high priest, establishes a Greek gymnasium in Jerusalem; Jews engage in nude Greek athletic contests, even attempting to reverse circumcisions.

167–164 BCE A family of priests leads a revolt against the Hellenistic regime. Led by Judah Maccabee (the Hammer), they are successful in bringing religious freedom back to Judea.

37 BCE King Herod begins erecting sports stadiums in Judea, establishes Olympics every five years, and brings athletes from around the world to compete in them.

70 CE Romans defeat the Jewish revolt and raze the Second Temple and Jerusalem.

c. 73–74 CE The fighters at Masada, a fortress in the Judean Desert and the last stronghold of the Jewish revolt, commit mass suicide.

132 Bar Kochba leads a revolt of Jews against the Romans. Defeated in 135, many of the leaders are tortured in the Coliseum at Caesarea.

c. 200 Completion of the Mishnah, the rabbinic discussions which form the core of the Talmud; the laws cover every intimate aspect of life including sex, notably in the laws surrounding niddah, or the separation of men from menstruating women.

c. 250 Simon ben Lakish, a Jewish gladiator, catches a glimpse of Rabbi Yochanan bathing and is captivated; he marries Yochanan's sister and becomes a scholar.

1038 Shmuel HaNagid (Samuel the Prince) becomes Vizier of Granada and leads its armies in battle.

1138 Birth of Moses son of Maimon, later known as Maimonides, who will become the most famous of Jewish doctors and who celebrated the importance of health of the body as well as the mind.

c. 1270–1280 The *Zohar*, the primary text of Kabbalah, or Jewish mysticism, is composed in Gerona, Spain; Kabbalah ascribes powerful qualities to God, which can correspond with parts of the body.

1492 King Ferdinand and Queen Isabella, having united Spain under Christian rule, compel the Jews to leave Spain or convert to Christianity; those that stay are subject to the Inquisition, and many are executed as false converts.

c. 1515 Michaelangelo sculpts *Moses* for the tomb of Pope Julius; the horns, based on a fourth-century mistranslation by Jerome, enter anti-Semitic lore.

c. 1596 William Shakespeare writes *The Merchant of Venice*, famed for its depiction of

Shylock, the greedy Jew who insists on his "pound of flesh."

1609 Death of Rabbi Judah Loew of Prague (the Maharal) who, according to legend, built a golem—a kind of benign monster—to defend the Jews of his city.

1792 "Light of Israel" Daniel Mendoza becomes the sixteenth champion of the London Prize Ring.

1881–1882 Wave of violent pogroms sweeps through Russian empire, leading to mass emigration of Jews and founding of first Jewish self-defense groups.

1882 Emma Lazarus, in her "Epistle to the Hebrews," calls for Jews to regain physical strength and martial power.

1882 Members of *Hibbat Tziyon* (the Lovers of Zion) begin to immigrate to Israel in a movement that will become known as the First Aliyah.

1886 Rudolph Virchow, a great German physician and pioneer of public health, concludes that Jewish children are physically indistinguishable from non-Jewish children.

1896   Jacques Joseph (né Jakob Levin), a
       German Jewish physician, performs the
       first modern rhinoplasty.

1897   Theodor Herzl holds the first Zionist
       Congress in Basel; within a year, the
       emerging Zionist movement has eight
       hundred chapters across Europe,
       representing over 100,000 Jews.

1898   Max Nordau, at the Second Zionist
       Congress, advocates for a new race of
       Muskeljudentum, muscle-Jewry. With
       Max Mandelstam, he establishes bar
       Kochba clubs, or Maccabi clubs, a
       gymnastics club to enhance physical
       fitness among Jewish youth.

1904–1914   The Second Aliyah, a wave of immi-
       gration, brings 40,000 Jews, most of
       them from Russia, to the land of Israel.

1905   The first publication, in Russia, of the
       antisemitic forgery *The Protocols of the
       Elders of Zion*.

1905   Jewish physician Sigmund Freud pub-
       lishes his *Three Essays on the Theory of
       Sex*, analyzing the importance of bodily
       experience, desire, and the Oedipus
       complex.

1907 Jews in Palestine begin to defend settlements themselves, leading in 1909 to the creation of *HaShomer* (the Guard), a small guild of watchmen to guard Jewish settlements in Palestine.

1910 Founding of Degania, the first Kibbutz and a landmark event in the development of a new society in the land of Israel.

1913 Hadassah, the women's Zionist group founded by Henrietta Szold to relieve suffering among the Jews of Palestine, sends its first two nurses to open a clinic in Jerusalem.

1916 Kafka writes *The Metamorphosis*, a story of the body as a source of horror.

1916 Founding of HaShomer HaTzair, a Zionist-socialist youth movement that aimed to prepare European Jewish youth for Kibbutz life; inspired by HaShomer in Palestine but rejecting its military aspect.

1917 Ze'ev Jabotinsky organizes the Jewish Legion as part of the British army in World War I; he hopes it will eventually become a Jewish army that will defend the land of Israel.

October 1917   Several members of NILI, a secret group that spied on the Turks for the British during World War I, are caught by Turks; Sarah Aaronsohn, one of the group's most famed members, commits suicide after three days of torture.

November 2, 1917   The British government issues the Balfour Declaration promising "The establishment in Palestine of a national home for the Jewish people."

1932   The first Maccabiah games are played in Tel Aviv. Founded to promote physical strength and skill among Jews, the games brought many Jewish athletes to Palestine as immigrants; since the 1950s, the games have been held every four years, bringing Jewish athletes from around the world to Israel.

1934   Jewish boxer Barney Ross holds World Lightweight, World Junior Welterweight, and World Welterweight titles.

October 1934   Hank Greenberg, first baseman and star hitter for the Detriot Tigers, sits out an important game in order to observe Yom Kippur.

September 1935 Nazi Germany enacts the Nuremberg Laws, defining the Jews as a race, prohibiting marriage between Jews and non-Jews, and stripping German Jews of their citizenship.

1939–1945 The Nazi Holocaust (the Shoah) exterminates 6 million European Jews, among them 1.5 million children, and drives most survivors into exile.

1943 Josef Mengele appointed doctor of Auschwitz, where he conducts brutal experiments and sends many tens of thousands of Jews and other inmates to the gas chambers at Birkenau.

November 1944 Hannah Szenes, a Hungarian Jew who had emigrated to Palestine and then returned to Europe as part of a Haganah mission to rescue Jews, is executed.

1944–1945 Formation of the Jewish Brigade, combining preexisting Jewish units from the British armed forces into a unified command that fought in Europe, notably in Italy. The Brigade helped Shoah survivors in newly liberated Europe and provided a pool

of experienced fighters for the Israeli
Army.

1945 Bess Meyerson, a Jewish girl from New
York, wins the Miss America pageant,
showing that a Jew could achieve the
American ideal of beauty—if she
didn't look too Jewish.

May 14, 1948 The State of Israel is proclaimed; the
new country is immediately invaded
by six Arab armies.

June 4, 1948 Karola Ruth Siegel, later known as Dr.
Ruth, then a twenty-year-old sniper in
the Haganah, is badly injured in the
War of Independence.

1958 Publication of *Exodus*, by Leon Uris, a
novel celebrating the courage of Jewish
fighters in Israel's War of Independence.

1959 Philip Roth's *Goodbye, Columbus* brings
the Jewish body into mainstream
American literature.

1962 Publication of *Yentl* by Isaac Bashevis
Singer, in which a woman hides her
body so that she can study in a yeshiva
with men.

October 1965 Sandy Koufax, pitcher for the Los Angeles Dodgers, refuses to play in a World Series game on Yom Kippur.

June 1967 The Six-Day War, in which Israel soundly defeats vastly larger Arab armies, is a turning point in the general perception of Jews as strong fighters.

1968 Barbra Streisand wins the Academy Award for her portrayal of Jewish actress Fanny Brice in *Funny Girl*. Unlike Brice, who had cosmetic surgery in 1923, Streisand keeps her Jewish nose.

September 5, 1972 Eleven Israeli Olympians are taken hostage by Palestinian terrorists at the Munich Olympics; all are killed. Jewish swimmer Mark Spitz, having won a record seven gold medals, is escorted from Munich under high security after the attack.

1990 Geneticist Mary-Claire King identifies the BRCA1 gene for hereditary breast cancer; this gene has a high incidence among Ashkenazic Jews.

2003 Ilan Ramon, son of Holocaust survivors, becomes the first Israeli in space, taking with him a small Torah and a drawing of earth from space by a boy who died in the Holocaust, but he himself is killed when the shuttle explodes.

August 25, 2004 Gal Friedman wins Israel's first Olympic gold medal, in surfing.

2005 Researchers at the University of Utah suggest that the prevalence of genetic diseases among Jews may be linked to higher intelligence.

ABOUT THE AUTHOR

Melvin Konner, Ph.D., M.D., the author of nine books, is a Samuel Candler Dobbs Professor of Anthropology at Emory University in Atlanta, where he teaches in the anthropology, human biology, and Jewish studies programs. He has written for *The New York Times*, *The New York Times Magazine*, *Newsweek*, the *Los Angeles Times*, *Science*, *Nature*, and *The New England Journal of Medicine*. You can visit his Web site at www.jewsandothers.com.